Get started in Polish

Joanna Michalak-Gray

For UK order enquiries: please contact Bookpoint Ltd,
130 Milton Park, Abingdon, Oxon OX14 4SB.
Telephone: +44 (0) 1235 827720. *Fax:* +44 (0) 1235 400454.
Lines are open 09.00–17.00, Monday to Saturday, with a
24-hour message answering service. Details about our titles
and how to order are available at www.teachyourself.com

For USA order enquiries: please contact McGraw-Hill Customer
Services, PO Box 545, Blacklick, OH 43004-0545, USA.
Telephone: 1-800-722-4726. *Fax:* 1-614-755-5645.

For Canada order enquiries: please contact McGraw-Hill Ryerson Ltd,
300 Water St, Whitby, Ontario L1N 9B6, Canada.
Telephone: 905 430 5000. *Fax:* 905 430 5020.

Long renowned as the authoritative source for self-guided learning –
with more than 50 million copies sold worldwide – the *Teach Yourself*
series includes over 500 titles in the fields of languages, crafts, hobbies,
business, computing and education.

British Library Cataloguing in Publication Data: a catalogue record for
this title is available from the British Library.

Library of Congress Catalog Card Number: on file.

First published in UK 2009 as *Teach Yourself Beginner's Polish*
by Hodder Education, part of Hachette UK, 338 Euston Road,
London NW1 3BH.

First published in US 2009 as *Teach Yourself Beginner's Polish*
by The McGraw-Hill Companies, Inc.

This edition published 2010.

The *Teach Yourself* name is a registered trade mark of Hodder Headline.

Typeset by MPS Limited, a Macmillan Company.

Printed in Great Britain for Hodder Education, an Hachette
UK Company, 338 Euston Road, London NW1 3BH,
by CPI Cox & Wyman, Reading, Berkshire RG1 8EX.

The publisher has used its best endeavours to ensure that the URLs
for external websites referred to in this book are correct and active at
the time of going to press. However, the publisher and the author have
no responsibility for the websites and can make no guarantee that a
site will remain live or that the content will remain relevant, decent or
appropriate.

Hachette UK's policy is to use papers that are natural, renewable and
recyclable products and made from wood grown in sustainable forests.
The logging and manufacturing processes are expected to conform to
the environmental regulations of the country of origin.

Impression number	10 9 8 7 6 5 4 3 2
Year	2014 2013 2012 2011

Acknowledgements

I would like to thank my family, especially Ian for his patience, support and encouragement, friends too numerous to mention individually by name, in England and Poland for their direct and indirect contributions. A special thanks to Nigel Gotteri for his considerable contribution to this course and to Chris and Isla Adamek, Anna and Rob Marfleet, Helena McDougall and Brenda Rabbidge, for being enthusiastic students and patient recipients of all the good and not so good ideas which shaped this course. As always I owe a great debt of gratitude to the editors, particularly Alexandra Jaton, Helen Vick, Helen Hart and the reviewers.

Any flak should, of course, be directed straight at the author.

Contents

i

Credits

Front cover: © Adam Antolak/iStockphoto.com

Back cover and pack: © Jakub Semeniuk/iStockphoto.com,
© Royalty-Free/Corbis, © agencyby/iStockphoto.com, © Andy
Cook/iStockphoto.com, © Christopher Ewing/iStockphoto.com,
© zebicho – Fotolia.com, © Geoffrey Holman/iStockphoto.com,
© Photodisc/Getty Images, © James C. Pruitt/iStockphoto.com,
© Mohamed Saber – Fotolia.com

Pack: © Stockbyte/Getty Images

Meet the author

I started my teaching career some 30 years ago, in 1980, as a teacher of English as a foreign language in Poland. After ten years of teaching English to students of different backgrounds, ages and abilities I moved to Britain and switched to teaching Polish to English speaking students. The lack of appropriate textbooks persuaded me to start writing my own material and to develop a new approach to teaching Polish based on real-life conversations incorporated into story-like courses, combined with user-friendly grammar explanations.

I am co-author of **Complete Polish** and author of **Speak Polish with Confidence**, both published by Hodder Education. I also worked as a language consultant for **Last-Minute Polish** by Elisabeth Smith.

Since 1993, I have worked as a scrutineer of Polish GCSE examinations.

Joanna Michalak-Gray

Only got a minute?

Polish may sometimes be perceived as a somewhat obscure language but it is the native language of Nicholas Copernicus, Joseph Conrad, Maria Curie and Frederic Chopin, and the adopted language of the eminent historian Professor Norman Davies and the famous violinist Nigel Kennedy. Its grammar and lexicon reflects the complex history and character of Poland – a place straddling East and West, Latin and Christian on the one hand, while influenced by the Ottoman Empire on the other. In the past, Poland was at the crossroads of trade routes – mainly the Amber Route leading from the Baltic Sea to the Mediterranean and linking with the Silk Route. Religious and political tolerance, as well as liberal laws, attracted merchants and artists from all over Europe and the Middle East who enriched the Polish language with words of Turkish, Mongolian, Jewish, Russian, German, Italian or French origin.

But above all, the story of the Polish language is the story of survival against all the odds – from the day when Poland ceased to exist on the map of Europe in 1795, when it was partitioned between the three powers of Russia, Prussia and the Austro-Hungarian Empire, through the days of national uprisings and the determination of the occupying powers to eradicate Polish altogether, both world wars and the age of Orwellian New Speak of the communist regime – the language and the people survived. Far from being eradicated, Polish has produced many great works of literature including being internationally acclaimed through four Noble Prize winners (Henryk Sienkiewicz, Władysław Reymont, Czesław Miłosz, Wisława Szymborska). Learning Polish is exciting and challenging but ultimately extremely rewarding – it will open and expand your horizons beyond anything you thought was possible.

5 Only got five minutes?

It may sound rather surprising but Polish and English have actually got quite a lot in common – both languages belong to the same broad family of Indo-European languages, both have been heavily influenced by Latin and Greek, and Polish has adopted a lot of English vocabulary. Words such as **muzyka, matematyka, medycyna, filozofia, fizyka** or **komputer** will not be difficult to figure out.

Words of Latin origin which in English end in -*tion*, in Polish end in **-cja**. For example, *information* – **informacja**, *adoration* – **adoracja**, *congregation* – **kongregacja**, *inflation* – **inflacja**, *foundation* – **fundacja**.

Similarily, where English words end in -*al*, Polish counterparts end in **-iczny**. For example, *political* – **polityczny**, *musical* – **muzyczny**, *logical* – **logiczny**, *medical* – **medyczny**.

But Polish and English are also similar in another way. Like English today, Polish used to be the lingua-franca of the Central and Eastern Europe at the time of the Polish–Lithuanian Commonwealth.

There are many differences of course, but it is always helpful to focus on the common ground and take it from there. So what is Polish really like? Is it as difficult as many claim it to be? What about its tounge-twisting pronunciation? And what about its history?

Polish with Czech and Slovak belongs to West-Slavonic languages. Its history goes back to approximately the 10th century when in 966 Duke Mieszko I, the ruler of several newly united Polish tribes accepted Christianity. With Christianity came Latin. Adopting the Latin alphabet allowed Polish to develop into a written form and opened Poland to Western ideas. The establishment of the Jagiellonian University in Kraków in 1364 further nurtured links between scholars in Poland and those of other great medieval European universities.

With the advent of the Polish–Lithuanian Commonwealth, a Golden Age dawned and with it a new importance for Polish – it became a lingua-franca of Central Europe. The Polish kingdom stretched from the Baltic to the Black Sea; its tolerance and liberal laws attracted merchants and artists from all over Europe as well as refugees fleeing poverty and persecution in other European countries. This fact is rather surprising considering that in modern times it is the Poles who have frequently become immigrants themselves.

But by 1795 the glory days were over. Poland was partitioned and removed from the map of Europe, while the Polish language was deliberately pushed out of public life with the full intention of making it extinct. The plan did not work though, and the more the occupying powers tried to diminish Polish, the harder Poles resisted any such move. However, over 120 years of partitions left their mark on the language which absorbed some German and Russian influences.

The end of World War I brought independence for Poland and the freedom to use Polish as an official language in public life again. But yet again history intervened and within the space of 30 years Poles who wanted to study their native language would have to do so in secrecy, risking their lives. World War II brought the German occupation of Poland, unimaginable distruction and an attempt to relegate Polish to the status of a second class language. The end of World War II heralded the emergence of communism with its Orwellian New Speak. The Polish language was transformed to serve the new reality.

The collapse of communism in 1989 and the emergence of the market economy meant that new words describing consumer products never seen in Poland before had to be introduced, and they had to be introduced fast. The frantic pace of the development of new technologies demanded the language to keep up. This time it was English which had the strongest impact on Polish.

For many Poles their language is a precious thing – it's a symbol of Polish survival; always closely linked to the fortunes of the country and the nation, used as an instrument of oppresion, indoctrination and power, as well as the medium to express the most patriotic ideas. It is probably the most important factor in shaping what Poland and the Poles are like today.

How to use this book

Learning a foreign language is always exciting, but learning on your own can also be daunting. There are no fellow students or tutors to support you. I hope **Get Started in Polish** will make the task of learning Polish alone a lot less daunting and much more enjoyable than it might be. To help you on your way, I have included bilingual dialogues, and exercises that can be turned into a game which can be played as a group activity or alone. Also included is cultural information about Poland together with lots of useful learning tips.

Dialogues are bilingual, with Polish and English side by side. This layout gives you full control over the text and removes ambiguity; you always know what's going on in the dialogue. It also gives you an opportunity to learn phrases in context. Don't be afraid to learn the whole dialogue by heart like a poem or nursery rhyme. One of the best ways to work with dialogues is to copy them carefully onto individual pieces of paper (a good writing exercise in itself), mix the pieces up and put the dialogue together again. Another way is to mask the Polish side of the dialogue and translate the English part into Polish. Then you can swap sides to practise translation from Polish into English.

Each Dialogue is proceeded by a **Vocabulary box** which lists all the new vocabulary introduced in the Dialogue. You may be puzzled by the fact that in the middle column of each vocabulary table some words appear in pairs separated by a symbol >. The words in question will always be verbs and the two varieties represent perfective and imperfective forms of these verbs. This book systematically puts imperfective verbs first and perfective second (which is what most books do), and backs this up with a little arrowhead (>) pointing away from the imperfective verb and towards the perfective. Although the system is used right from the start you will find a full explanation in Unit 12.

Diagrams are provided to help you absorb and organize the words, expressions and phrases you've just learned in the dialogues. They can be copied onto pieces of paper (index cards, sticky-notes, cards, etc.)

and displayed on any flat surface in the same way as they appear in the book. You can put them on walls, a fridge, kitchen cupboard doors, mirrors, office board, in fact anywhere where you can see them while doing other things. They just need to be visible and accessible. Learning a language doesn't always mean opening a textbook and swotting for hours. You can learn a language in the most unconventional situations.

The **exercises** in the **Test yourself** sections follow a certain pattern, translations (sentences into Polish or into English), language use (completing sentences), and communication (responding in Polish to the prompts provided). You can turn them into a language learning game. You will find the board and the rules of the game at the end of the book.

The **language game** is optional; it can be played solo or with learning partners, with or without a board, for three minutes or for three hours. The learner is in control. The game consists of a collection of small cards in different colours (blue, green, yellow and purple). Each colour denotes a different type of task.

You are encouraged to make your own cards because it's a good writing exercise. One side of the card contains the question while the answer (taken from the **Key to the exercises**) can be written on the reverse (this way you can assess yourself). At the early stages you can simply collect cards and if you keep them close by you can spend five, ten or 15 minutes going over the cards every day while waiting for bus, on the train or at coffee breaks. You can do it any time and anywhere and there's no need to have a textbook with you. Successful learning depends on repetition and revision and the cards are great help in doing so. In the later stages, when you have enough cards to start using the board you can make your own board using the template included in the textbook (it needs to be adapted because black and white print will only allow two colours). Again, the game can be played by one as well as many players. The game is in addition to and not instead of something else. Playing the game will enhance the learning experience, but not playing the game will not stop you from effective learning.

The answers to all the exercises are in the **Key to the exercises** at the back of the book, but most of the exercises, along with the correct answers are also on the recording.

Although there is a brief general introduction to Polish pronunciation at the beginning of the book, each Unit also contains a **Pronunciation guide** which will guide you step by step through Polish pronunciation and will enable you to practise it as much as you need.

At the end of the book you'll find a **Grammar appendix** in which all the grammatical and linguistic material discussed in the course is gathered, and some additional points explained. Following that are **Test yourself revision exercises** which provide a further opportunity to practise more of what you have learned in this course.

There is also a **Taking it further** section with useful information if you would like to continue your study or if you are interested in finding out more about Poland. You will also find a **Polish–English vocabulary** and **English–Polish vocabulary** at the back of the book.

Symbols used in the course

Although you can study without a recording, the course is best used with the accompanying recording. Look out for the ◀ symbol which indicates that the text is recorded.

Author insight boxes give you additional advice on strategies on how to improve your learning skills to get the best out of the course.

Above all, I hope that you'll enjoy learning Polish and that in doing so you'll develop your own exciting story.

◀ **CD1, TR 1**

Pronunciation guide

Polish has a reputation for being a language with difficult grammar and even more difficult pronunciation. With the recent influx of Poles to the UK and other countries as well as millions of tourist and business people visiting Poland every year, a lot of people who face the need to pronounce Polish names like Leszczyński, Trzebniewski, Grzegorzewski or Tchórzewski would concur with that view. Yet things are not as they might seem. Polish words may look daunting to an English speaker's eye, but once you've learned some ground rules, you'll be delighted to discover how consistent Polish pronunciation is. In huge contrast to the situation in English, you'll immediately be able to pronounce Polish words when you see them for the first time. This includes the names of Polish people and places, however obscure; as long as you don't panic and don't rush, you'll be fine. Because this consistency works so much in your favour as a learner, Polish pronunciation is covered in quite a lot of detail throughout the course. We will start with the general introduction here but you will find a section called **Pronunciation guide** *Jak to wymówić?* in each unit, which is also supported by the recording.

Polish, like English, uses the Latin alphabet. Compared to English, *q, v* and *x* are missing from normal Polish spelling, but the total number of letters in the Polish alphabet is brought up from a mere 23 (English's 26 minus three) to 32 by extra letters with squiggles: an acute accent over, a tail under, a line through or a dot over:

ą, ć, ę, ł, ń, ó, ś, ź, ż

The letters **ą** and **ę** can be described as **a z ogonkiem** and **e z ogonkiem** (*with a little tail*). The final letters of the Polish alphabet are **ź** [ziet] or **zet z kreską** (*zed with an accent*) and **ż** [żet] or **zet z kropką** (*zed with a dot*). The acute accent ´ is known as **kreska** in Polish, so **ć**, etc. can be described as **z kreską** (*with an accent*).

Remember that the **kreska** (acute accent) ´ does not indicate stress or emphasis.

Here is the order of the Polish alphabet:

a, ą, b, c, ć, d, e, ę, f, g, h, i, j, k, l, ł, m, n, ń, o, ó, p, r, s, ś, t, u, w, y, z, ź, ż

Each of the letters represents a distinct sound of its own, apart from **ó** and **u**, which represent exactly the same sound. The two letters with tails (**z ogonkiem**) can represent a succession of two sounds.

Sometimes a pair of letters represents a single sound: **ch, cz, dz, dż, rz,** sz. (you'll find a more detailed explanation of how these are pronounced later in Unit 5).

Stress (emphasis, accent) almost always falls on the last syllable but one of a word. Exceptions like **Ameryka**, where the accent is put on the third syllable from the end [a-**me**-ry-ka], abbreviations and certain verb forms will be noted in Unit 9.

Points to bear in mind:

- ▶ Polish stress (emphasis on a particular part of a word) is quite light.
- ▶ Unstressed syllables are pronounced as clearly as stressed ones (a help when you're learning endings).

The most important thing to remember about Polish intonation is that statements in which your voice falls towards the end of a sentence can be turned into questions just by raising the pitch of your voice at the end.

We will develop all these points, and more, as we go along in each unit.

1

Jestem Andrew
I'm Andrew

In this unit you will learn
- *how to introduce yourself*
- *how to state your nationality and profession*
- *how to address somebody politely*
- *how to say you are hungry or tired*

'To be or not to be' could be an alternative title for this unit. Expressing who you are or are not, what your profession is or isn't, what you are like and how you feel, are the most useful basic sentences in any language and Polish is no exception. You can express all of these things using just the verb **być** *to be* and in this unit you will learn how. You will also learn how to greet somebody in Polish, how to invite somebody in and how to address Poles politely.

Dialogue 1 **Dialog pierwszy**

Andrew Stewart, a British detective, is visiting Poland. He is trying to trace his family roots. He's visiting Maria Grajewska, a retired archivist who runs a specialist website for people interested in genealogy. Andrew and Maria have been in touch over the Internet but have never met face to face. Maria opens the door. Andrew has learned some Polish in the past and is keen to try it out.

Vocabulary Słówka

Form (as it appears) in the dialogue	Basic form (dictionary form)	English translation
dzień		*day*
dobry		*good*
pani		*Madam/Mrs/Ms, lady*
panu	pan	*Sir/Mr, gentleman*
jestem	być *to be*	*I'm*
bardzo		*very*
Bardzo mi miło.	ja, miły	*Pleased to meet you.*
proszę	prosić > poprosić*	*please*
wejść		*come in/go in*

*Many Polish verbs have two 'versions' to reflect their *perfective* and *imperfective* forms. Although it is too early in the course to explain exactly what these forms are, they will be nevertheless indicated in Vocabulary boxes right from the start. The rule is that the imperfective form appears first with the arrowhead symbol > pointing towards the perfective form. It will all become clear in Unit 12 where perfective and imperfective forms are explained in detail.

Andrew	Dzień dobry pani.	*Good morning, (madam).*
	Jestem Andrew Stewart.	*I'm Andrew Stewart.*
Maria	Dzień dobry panu.	*Good morning, (sir).*
	Jestem Maria Grajewska.	*I'm Maria Grajewska.*
Andrew	Bardzo mi miło.	*Pleased to meet you.*
Maria	Proszę wejść.	*Do come in.*

CD1, TR 2, 01.34

Polish surnames

A lot of typical Polish surnames end in -**ski** or -**cki** for men and -**ska** or -**cka** for women. For example:

Tomasz Grajewski	Maria Grajewska
Lech Kaczyński	Ewa Kaczyńska
Krzysztof Kieślowski	Barbara Kieślowska
Edward Forsycki	Danuta Forsycka

Polish distinguishes masculine and feminine surnames like these by giving them different endings.

How to address Poles by name

Poles maintain three broad levels of formality in the way they address each other by name:

1 The most formal of all, very official, using **pan** *Sir* or **pani** *Ms/Mrs* + surname to address people they don't know.
    pan (Jan) Grajewski/pani (Maria) Grajewska

2 Less formal, quite neutral, using **pan/pani** + first name to address somebody they know but they are not close friends or relatives, or haven't got permission to address them by their first name. Colleagues at work would often use this form.
    pan Jan/pani Maria

3 Informal, using just the first name, often in its diminutive (affectionate) form, to address somebody they are related to, or know very well, or in the case of young children.
    Maria/Marysia/Marysieńka
    Barbara/Basia/Basieńka
    Małgorzata/Małgosia/Gosia/Gośka
    Jan/Janek/Jasiek/Jaś
    Andrzej/Jędrek

Pan and *Pani*

Andrew uses **pani** when addressing Maria. They don't really know each other yet and saying 'Good morning madam' is an appropriate thing to do. (Not that English uses *sir* or *madam* much, but in this book those two words occur a lot, to remind you that Polish indicates gender, and that the form being used in Polish is not the familiar one.)

Dialogue 2 **Dialog drugi**

Andrew comes in. Pani Maria invites him to sit down and asks if he's tired. He is, a bit. Pani Maria also enquires if he's hungry.

Vocabulary **Słówka**

Form (as it appears) in the dialogue	Basic form (dictionary form)	English translation
usiąść	siadać > usiąść	*to sit down*
czy		*word used to introduce a yes/no question*
jest	być	*s/he/it* is*
zmęczony	męczyć > zmęczyć	*tired*
tak		*yes*
trochę		*a little bit*
a		*and/but*
głodny		*hungry*
nie		*no/not*

*From now on, *he/she/it* will be abbreviated to *s/he/it*.

Maria	Proszę usiąść.	*Please sit down./Do sit down.*
	Czy jest pan zmęczony?	*Are you tired?*
Andrew	Tak, trochę.	*Yes, a bit.*
Maria	A czy jest pan głodny?	*And are you hungry?*
Andrew	Nie. Nie jestem głodny.	*No. I'm not hungry.*

Dialogue 3 **Dialog trzeci**

Pani Maria is curious as to Andrew's nationality. She asks whether he's English or Scottish.

Vocabulary **Słówka**

Form (as it appears) in the dialogue	Basic form (dictionary form)	English translation
Szkotem	Szkot	*Scot(sman)*
czy		*or; is also used to introduce a question with a yes/no answer*

i		*and*
Anglikiem	Anglik	*Englishman*
Polką	Polka	*Polish woman*
szkockie korzenie	szkocki, korzeń	*Scottish roots*

Maria	Czy jest pan Szkotem czy Anglikiem?	*Are you Scottish or English?*
Andrew	Jestem pół Szkotem i pół Anglikiem. A pani? Czy pani jest Polką?	*I'm half Scottish and half English. And (what about) you? Are you Polish?*
Maria	Tak, jestem Polką, ale mam szkockie korzenie.	*Yes, I'm Polish, but I've got Scottish roots.*

Dialogue 4 **Dialog czwarty**

Andrew wants to know what Pani Maria does for a living.

Vocabulary **Słówka**

Form (as it appears) in the dialogue	Basic form (dictionary form)	English translation
Czym się pan/pani zajmuje?		*What do you do for a living?/ What are you doing?*
emerytką	emerytka	*retired woman*
prywatnym	prywatny	*private*
detektywem	detektyw	*detective*
naprawdę		*really*

Andrew	Czym się pani zajmuje?	*What do you do (for a living)?*
Maria	Jestem emerytką. A pan?	*I'm retired. And you?*
Andrew	Jestem prywatnym detektywem.	*I'm a private detective.*
Maria	Naprawdę?	*Really?*

Listen to the dialogues several times until you feel confident you understand them well. Don't feel disheartened when, initially, the conversation seems to be just a string of unrecognizable sounds. After listening to the text several times you will begin to hear when one word ends and another begins. After a few more times you will be able to understand everything that is said. And finally, you will feel confident enough to repeat whole sentences.

Let's practise

▶ Separate Polish from English translations.
▶ Copy the dialogues (both Polish and English parts) onto individual pieces of paper.
▶ Mix the pieces and reconstruct the dialogues (again both parts) correctly.
▶ Mix the pieces again and reconstruct only the Polish side of the dialogues.

How the language works

Word endings

Basic sentences like **Jestem Anglikiem** *I'm an Englishman*, **Jestem Polką** *I'm Polish* (woman), **Jestem zmęczony** *I'm tired* (man) and **Jestem głodna** *I'm hungry* (woman) illustrate one of the fundamental principles of Polish: that words have different endings. These endings show what a word is doing in relation to others in the sentence. Let me explain.

Words like **detektyw** (*detective*), **emerytka** (*retired woman*), **Polka** (*Polish woman*) and **Anglik** (*Englishman*) are nouns. Nouns are used, for example, to refer to things, animals, natural world phenomena, concepts and people. Other examples of nouns in English are *book, tiger, volcano, happiness, teacher, laughter*, etc. In Polish, nouns belong to one of three genders: masculine, feminine or neuter.

For example, if you're a woman and Polish, your nationality noun will be **Polka**. If you are a man and Polish, your nationality noun will be **Polak**.

The ending of these words will change if you use them with a word like **Jestem** (*I'm*):

Jestem Polką.	*I'm Polish. (woman)*
Jestem Polakiem.	*I'm Polish. (man)*
Jestem Angielką.	*I'm English. (woman)*
Jestem Anglikiem.	*I'm English. (man)*

As you see, Polish distinguishes 'genders'. The main thing to realize about gender in languages like Polish is that it is not just a matter of sex. In Polish, not only people have gender; things are also masculine, feminine or neuter, depending on what word is used to refer to them. For example, **księżyc** (*moon*) is masculine and so is **statek** (*ship*) but **radio** (*radio*), **mleko** (*milk*) and **piwo** (*beer*) are all neuter.

How do you recognize whether a noun is masculine, feminine or neuter? More often than not, by its ending. Most masculine nouns end in a consonant (represented by a letter other than the vowel letters **a, e, i, o, u, y**), most feminine nouns end in **-a**, and most neuter nouns end in **-o** or **-e**.

The gender will also dictate how other words, such as adjectives, behave. Adjectives are closely related to nouns because they are the words that modify the meaning of nouns: a *big* house, a *new* car, a *tired* detective, a *hungry* woman, etc. In fact, adjectives work so closely with nouns that in Polish they adapt themselves to the gender of the nouns they accompany. So if the noun is masculine, the adjective will also be in its masculine form; if the noun is feminine, the adjective is also in its feminine form, and so on. This is what you saw happening with Mr Kowalski and Mrs Kowalska; to a Pole, they obviously have the same surname, a fact which might need explaining to others. Adjectives in their masculine form typically end in **-y**, adjectives in their feminine form end in **-a** and adjectives in their neuter form end in **-e**.

Andrew is a man, so he introduces and describes himself like this:

Jestem Anglikiem.	I'm English.
Jestem detektywem.	I'm a detective.
Jestem zmęczony.	I'm tired.

On the other hand, if pani Maria were English, retired and tired she would say:

Jestem Angielką.	I'm English.
Jestem emerytką.	I'm retired.
Jestem zmęczona.	I'm tired.

To be być

Być albo nie być – oto jest pytanie!

In the dialogues you've come across two forms of the verb **być** *to be*: **jestem** (*I am*) and **jest** (*s/he/it is*). But what about the rest? Here's the full set. Pronouns (I, you, he, etc.) are given to help you match them to the verb forms, but **jestem**, for example, already means *I am*; you only need to include **ja** if you want to emphasize it, as in *It's me that's Polish*. This is particularly relevant in the case of the s/he/it forms, where the context may not make clear whether you mean he, she or it; the inclusion of **on**, **ona** or **ono** will clear up (and even emphasize) which you mean.

◀) **CD1, TR 6**

Singular				
ja	*I*	jestem	*am*	Jestem zmęczony/zmęczona. *I am tired.*
ty	*you*	jesteś	*are*	Jesteś zmęczony/zmęczona. *You are tired.*
on	*he*	jest	*is*	On jest zmęczony. *He is tired.*
ona	*she*	jest	*is*	Ona jest zmęczona. *She is tired.*
*ono	*it*	jest	*is*	Ono jest zmęczone. *It is tired.*
pan, pani	*you (sir, madam)*	jest		Pan jest zmęczony. *You (sir) are tired.* Pani jest zmęczona. *You (madam) are tired.*

Plural				
my	*we*	jesteśmy	*are*	Jesteśmy zmęczeni/zmęczone. *We are tired.*
wy	*you*	jesteście	*are*	Jesteście zmęczeni/zmęczone. *You are tired.*

*oni	they (including masculines)	są	are	Oni są zmęczeni. *They are tired.*
*one	they (not including masculines)	są	are	One są zmęczone. *They are tired.*
panowie	gentlemen			Panowie są zmęczone. *You are tired, gentlemen.* *You are tired, ladies.*
panie,	ladies,	są	are	Panie są zmęczeni.
państwo	you (gentlemen, ladies, ladies & gentlemen)	są	are	Państwo są zmęczeni. *You are tired, (ladies and gentlemen).*

*The pronoun **ono** is used for any neuter person (e.g. *a child*; **dziecko** is a neuter noun) or object.

Oni is either used for a group of men or a group of men and women.

One is used only for a group of women.

Listen and repeat

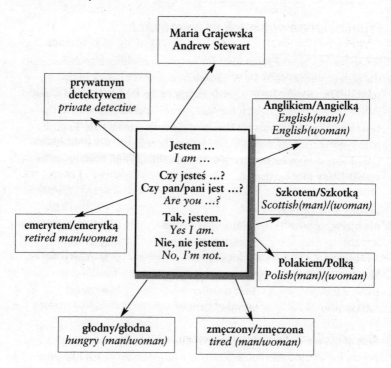

```
                    ┌─────────────────────┐
                    │  Maria Grajewska     │
                    │  Andrew Stewart      │
                    └─────────────────────┘
```

prywatnym
detektywem
private detective

Anglikiem/Angielką
English(man)/
English(woman)

Jestem …
I am …

Czy jesteś …?
Czy pan/pani jest …?
Are you …?

Szkotem/Szkotką
Scottish(man)/(woman)

Tak, jestem.
Yes I am.
Nie, nie jestem.
No, I'm not.

emerytem/emerytką
retired man/woman

Polakiem/Polką
Polish(man)/(woman)

głodny/głodna
hungry (man/woman)

zmęczony/zmęczona
tired (man/woman)

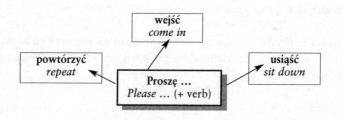

wejść
come in

powtórzyć
repeat

Proszę …
Please … (+ verb)

usiąść
sit down

Pronunciation guide **Jak to wymówić?**

Polish has acquired a reputation for notoriously difficult pronunciation through sentences such as: **W Szczebrzeszynie chrząszcz brzmi w trzcinie** (*In Szczebrzeszyn a beetle buzzes in the reeds*). This is a famous Polish tongue twister, which for many years held the top spot in the Guinness World Records for the most difficult sentence for English native speakers. However, the fact is that there are plenty of words in Polish that don't look terrifying to the uninitiated and don't cause English speakers any problems at all.

Listen and repeat

problem *problem*	telefon *telephone*	dokument *document*
kot *cat*	komputer *computer*	mapa *map*
lampa *lamp*	mama *mum*	plan *plan*
katedra *cathedral*	tato *dad*	dom *house*
okno *window*	brat *brother*	bilet *ticket*
radio *radio*	numer *number*	

One of the reasons why many words don't pose any pronunciation problems is that some Polish letters are pronounced much like their English counterparts:

b, d, f, g, k, l, m, n, p, s, t, z

It's worth remembering that **p**, **t** and **k** should be pronounced without the puff of air that usually follows them in English. *Poland* is **Polska**, not [P-holska]!

The **l** sound in Polish is generally similar to the sound at the beginning of the word *little*.

Insight

To be ...

Andrew is a detective and Maria is retired, but what about other professions, nationalities and conditions?

Nationalities		Professions		State we are in	
Male	Female	Male	Female	Male	Female
Anglik (English)	Angielka	lekarz (doctor)	lekarka	zmęczony (tired)	zmęczona
Szkot (Scottish)	Szkotka	aktor (actor)	aktorka	głodny (hungry)	głodna
Walijczyk (Welsh)	Walijka	student (student)	studentka	zajęty (busy)	zajęta
Irlandczyk (Irish)	Irlandka			pracowity (hard working)	pracowita
Polak (Pole)	Polka			dobry (good)	dobra

... or not to be

Negation in Polish works simply and consistently. Most of the time you put **nie** before the verb. Look at the following examples:

Jestem zmęczony/na.	I'm tired (man/woman).
Nie jestem zmęczony/na.	I'm not tired.
Jestem Walijczykiem.	I'm Welsh (a Welshman).
Nie jestem Walijczykiem.	I'm not Welsh.

Expressing a person's nationality

You will have noticed that nationality nouns like **Polak**, **Szkot** and **Anglik**, rather than adjectives like **polski**, **szkocki** and **angielski** are used when identifying someone by nationality:

Jestem Amerykaninem.	*I'm (an) American.*
Jestem Polakiem.	*I'm Polish./I'm a Pole.*

Test yourself

Exercise 1

Complete the following sentences by choosing the correct ending.

  a Ewa says: Jestem (Polakiem/Polką).
  b Patrick says: Jestem (Irlandczykiem/Irlandką).
  c Maria says: Jestem (pracowity/pracowita).
  d Tom says: Jestem (zajęty/zajęta).

Exercise 2

Choose the correct form.

  a Pani Maria is tired: Jest głodna/zmęczona/zmęczony.
  b Andrew is English: Jest Szkotem/Angielką/Anglikiem.
  c Pani Maria is retired: Jest emerytem/emerytką/detektywem.

Exercise 3

Look at the endings of the following words and say whether each one is masculine, feminine or neuter.

lampa *lamp*, samochód *car*, radio *radio*, telefon *telephone*, herbata *tea*, kobieta *woman*, dziecko *child*, dom *house*, autobus *bus*, tramwaj *tram*, tulipan *tulip*, mapa *map*, piwo *beer*

Exercise 4

Translate the following sentences into Polish and practise the pronunciation by saying them out loud. Check your pronunciation by playing the recording.

a Good morning/afternoon.
b Pleased to meet you.
c I'm Maria Grajewska.
d Please come in.
e Please sit down.
f Are you tired, sir?
g I'm not hungry.
h Are you Scottish, English or Polish? (to a man)
i What do you do for a living? (to a woman)
j I'm retired. (a woman)
k I'm English and a private detective. (a man)

Exercise 5

Choose the correct form in the sentences below. Again, try to say the correct answer out loud.

a Maria is Polish. Is she **Polską/Polką/Polak**?
b Andrew is English. Is he **Szkotem/Anglikiem/Angielką**?
c Maria is retired. Is she **emerytem/emerytką/prywatnym detektywem**?
d Maria invites Andrew to come in. Does she say **Proszę wejść/Proszę wyjść/Proszę usiąść**?

◆⁾ **CD 1, TR 9**

Exercise 6

Respond in Polish to the following questions and statements. To make the task easier we have given you prompts in English. Listen to the recording to check your answers.

a Dzień dobry, Jestem Ewa Borowska.
(Pleased to meet you.)
b Proszę usiąść.
(Thank you.)
c Czy jest pan zmęczony?
(Yes, a bit.)
d Czym się pan zajmuje?
(I'm retired.)

Did you know?

▶ Geographically, Poland is not in Eastern Europe. It is in central Europe.

▶ Poland is over 1,000 years old. Its formal creation was in the year 966 when the ruling prince, Mieszko I, decided to adopt Christianity as the official religion of his people, thus establishing political bonds with the rest of civilized Europe. Gniezno, a small town in Western Poland, was the first capital of Poland.

▶ The word 'Poland' – **Polonia** in Latin and **Polska** in Polish – comes from the name of the tribe 'Polanie' who used to inhabit the western part of today's country. It used to mean 'people living in open fields'.

2

To jest mój pies, Azor
This is my dog, Azor

In this unit you will learn
- **how to introduce others**
- **how to talk about family**
- **how to ask about and describe people, animals and objects**

You now know how to introduce yourself; it's time to learn how to introduce others. In this unit you'll also learn how to describe people, animals and objects.

Dialogue 1 **Dialog pierwszy**

Andrew and Maria are talking when suddenly Andrew hears a noise. He turns round and sees a dog coming into the living room. Maria explains it's her dog, Azor.

Vocabulary **Słówka**

Form in the dialogue	Dictionary form	English translation
to jest	być *(to be)*	*this is, it's*
mój		*my* (used with masc. nouns)
pies		*dog*
zły		*bad, angry, malicious* (here: aggressive)

nie	no
dobry	good

Maria	To jest mój pies, Azor.	*This is my dog, Azor.*
Andrew	Czy to jest zły pies?	*Is he an aggressive dog?*
Maria	Nie! Azor to jest bardzo dobry pies.	*No! Azor's a very good dog.*

Dialogue 2 **Dialog drugi**

Andrew and Maria resume their interrupted conversation. Andrew shows Maria some family photographs and explains who is in the photographs.

Vocabulary **Słówka**

Form in the dialogue	Dictionary form	English translation
moja	mój	*my (fem.)*
rodzina		*family*
żona		*wife*
ładna	ładny	*pretty*
córka		*daughter*
studentką	studentka	*female student*
studiuje	studiować	*s/he studies, is a student of*
medycynę	medycyna	*medicine*
Kto?		*Who?*
Kto to jest?		*Who is it? Who's this/that?*
ojciec		*father*

Andrew	To jest moja rodzina. Moja żona, Jenny.	*This is my family. My wife, Jenny.*
Maria	Jest bardzo ładna.	*She's very pretty.*

18

Andrew	A to jest moja córka, Molly. Jest studentką.	*And this is my daughter, Molly. She's a student.*
Maria	Co studiuje?	*What does she study? (What subject?)*
Andrew	Medycynę.	*Medicine.*
Maria	A kto to jest?	*And who's this?*
Andrew	To jest mój ojciec, Thomas.	*My father, Thomas.*

My family and other animals

There is a slight difference in what the word **rodzina** *family* means in English and in Polish. In English it usually means *children*. If you are asked: 'Have you got any family?' it's another way of asking: 'Have you got any children?'.

When you ask a Pole **Czy masz rodzinę?** *Have you got a family?* s/he will start a long litany of parents, grandparents, siblings, nieces, nephews and cousins, sometimes many times removed.

Although a lot of Poles keep animals, they aren't a nation of great animal lovers. Many dogs are kept for protection of property rather than companionship. That's why notices on gates often say:

Uwaga!

Zły pies!

Attention!

Aggressive (bad/angry/malicious) dog!

(Beware of the dog!)

Dialogue 3 Dialog trzeci

Andrew looks at the photographs on the wall. He asks Maria who the people in them are.

Vocabulary **Słówka**

Form in the dialogue	Dictionary form	English translation
Kto		*Who*
dziadek		*grandfather*
A to?		*And (what about) this?*
Mama		*Mum*

Andrew	Kto to jest?	*Who is it?*
Maria	To jest mój dziadek, Tomasz.	*This is my grandfather, Tomasz.*
Andrew	A to?	*And this?*
Maria	To jest moja mama, Teresa.	*This is my Mum, Teresa.*
Andrew	A to? Kto to jest?	*And this? Who's this?*
Maria	To jest mój ojciec, Jakub.	*This is my father, Jakub.*

Insight

Before you move on, listen to and practise the dialogues several times, until you feel confident.

Let's practise

► Copy the dialogues (both Polish and English parts) onto a small pieces of paper.
► Mix the pieces and reconstruct the dialogues correctly (both parts).
► Mix the pieces again and reconstruct the Polish side of the dialogues.
► Separate the Polish and English parts of the dialogues. Turn the Polish parts face down and mix them again. Turn them face up at random and translate into English.
► Do the same exercise with the English part of the dialogues.

You know who I'm talking about

Because Polish verbs have a unique ending for each person, **jestem** for *I*, **jesteś** for *you*, **jest** for *s/he*, it and so on, it's not necessary to use a personal pronoun (words like I, you, he, she etc.) to know who you're talking about. That's why we can say about Andrew: **Jest głodny**. We don't have to use **on**, *he*, as **jest** is a *s/he/it* (**on(a/o)**) form and the masculine form of the adjective **głodny** clearly indicates a male.

◆ **CD1, TR 13**

Listen and repeat

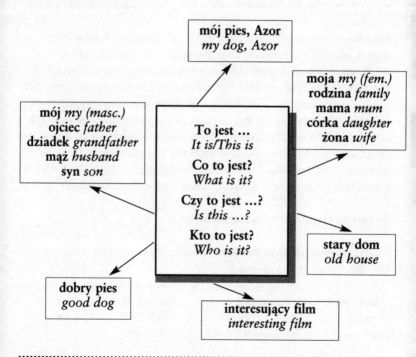

mój pies, Azor
my dog, Azor

moja *my (fem.)*
rodzina *family*
mama *mum*
córka *daughter*
żona *wife*

mój *my (masc.)*
ojciec *father*
dziadek *grandfather*
mąż *husband*
syn *son*

To jest ...
It is/This is

Co to jest?
What is it?

Czy to jest ...?
Is this ...?

Kto to jest?
Who is it?

stary dom
old house

dobry pies
good dog

interesujący film
interesting film

Insight

Copy the phrases above and put them on a flat surface where you can see them easily. Practise saying them out loud. Check the pronunciation on the recording.

How the language works

When you use the Polish word **to**, corresponding to English *this*, *that* or *it* with **jest** (or other forms of **być**) and a noun, the noun stays in the basic dictionary form (traditionally called the nominative). For example, **To jest detektyw** (*This is a detective*).

In fact, it's not unusual for **jest** to be left out, leaving just **to** and a nominative as in **To angielski detektyw**.

Why then does a word like **detektyw** stay in its basic dictionary form (nominative) in the sentence: **To jest detektyw** and changes when you say **Andrew jest detektywem?** It happens because in these two sentences **detektyw** plays a different role. In the first sentence you simply 'point and name' a noun. In the second sentence **detektyw** is used to complement (complete the meaning of) **być**. In other words, in the first case **detektyw** complements **to** and if you omit **jest** you will still understand the meaning of the sentence. In the second case **detektyw** complements **jest** and the sentence is not complete if one of them is omitted. Traditionally, the form (or case) of the noun which plays this role is called instrumental.

So how do I create an instrumental form?

Masculine nouns such as **detektyw** (ending in a consonant) add **-em** (or **-iem** if they end in **-g** or **-k**):

detektyw	*(detective)*	detektywem
student	*(male student)*	studentem
Polak	*(male Pole)*	Polakiem

Feminine (and some masculine exceptions) nouns ending in **-a** change to **-ą**:

emerytka	*(retired female)*	emerytką
studentka	*(female student)*	studentką
córka	*(daughter)*	córką

Neuter nouns lose their final **-o/-e** in favour of **-em** (or **-iem** after **-g** and **-k**):

piwo	*(beer)*	piwem
radio	*(radio)*	radiem

◀) **CD1, TR 15**

Pronunciation guide **Jak to wymówić?**

Vowels

Polish has nine vowels:
   a, ą, e, ę, i, o, ó, u, y

Let's have a closer look at what they represent:

▶ The letter **a** represents a sound midway between the *a* in *father* and the *a* in *bat* or *map*.

Listen and repeat the following examples: **mapa** *(map)*, **karta** *(menu)*, **Ala** *(female name)*, **lalka** *(doll)*.

▶ The letter **e** represents a sound like *e* in *bet* or *step*.

Listen and repeat: **Ewa** *(Eve)*, **meta** *(finish)*, **Europa** *(Europe)*, **energia** *(energy)*, **emerytka** *(retired female)*.

▶ The letter **i** represents a clear version of the long *i* sound in *clean*, *keen* or *knees*.

Listen and repeat: **bigos** *(hunter's stew)*, **Irena** *(Irene)*, **i** *(and)*, **igła** *(needle)*.

▶ The letter **o** is like the *o* in *box* or *pot*.

Listen and repeat these examples: **pot** *(sweat)*, **policja** *(police)*, **pogotowie** *(emergency service)*, **poczta** *(post office)*, **lokal** *(premises)*, **mleko** *(milk)*, **woda** *(water)*, **sok** *(juice)*.

▶ The letters **ó** and **u** both represent the same sound, e.g. the **ó** in **Bóg**, *God*, is similar to the *ou* in *you*.

Listen and repeat the examples: **kubek** (*mug*), **ulica** (*street*), **ósemka** (*the number eight*), **mucha** (*fly*).

▶ The letter **y** represents a sound like the short *i* in *bid* (but further away from the *i* in *bleed*).

Listen and repeat: **myć** (*to wash*), **być** (*to be*), **etykieta** (*etiquette*), **detektyw** (*detective*).

▶ The tailed nasal letters **ą** and **ę** sound like *o* as in *box* and *e* as in *bed*, lengthened by an *m* or some other nasal sound. Sometimes this is closer to an **n**, **m** or **ng**. Sometimes, especially before **ł** or at the end of words ending in **-ę**, the second element disappears altogether.

Listen and repeat the following words: **się** (ś-e) *oneself*, **będę** (bende) *I will be*, **parę** (pa-re) *a pair*, **kępę** (kempe) *a clump*.

Insight

All the exercises in the course can be turned into a game. You can find a board and the rules of the game at the end of the book. You will need a board, a pawn and a dice. You can copy the sentences in this exercise onto separate cards and mark them in a different colour according to the type of tasks they relate to. For example, the task in Exercise 1 relates to a translation from Polish into English. You can mark all the cards with that type of task in blue. Every time you land on a blue square on the game board you will need to draw a blue card and complete the task.

Test yourself

Exercise 1

Translate the following sentences into Polish and practise the pronunciation by saying them out loud.

a This is my dog, Toffee.
b He's a very good dog.
c Is this your *(twoja)* family?
d Yes, it's my wife and daughter.
e She's very pretty.
f Molly's a student.
g She studies medicine.
h Who's this?
i This is my grandfather, Jakub.
j Is this your mum?
k What is it?
l This is my family.

Exercise 2

Complete the following sentences. You can check your answers and pronunciation on the recording. (This exercise checks your grammatical knowledge of Polish. You can copy the sentences onto green cards for the game.)

a Moja córka jest (medycyna/ładna/zły).
b To jest moja (córka/pies/emerytką).
c To jest mój (pies/żona/zmęczony).
d Ona studiuje (ojciec/mama/medycynę).
e Azor to bardzo dobry (uwaga/dziadek/pies).

Exercise 3

Imagine a photograph of your immediate family. Think of how many family members you can now introduce, and do so in Polish. Listen to a sample answer on the recording.

◀) **CD1, TR 16**

Exercise 4

Respond in Polish to the following statements and questions. Again, check your answers and practice pronunciation of both questions and answers by listening to the recording. (This exercise relates to a communication task – you can copy both Polish sentences and English prompts onto yellow cards for the game.)

a Kto to jest?
  (*This is my father.*)
b Co studiuje twoja córka?
  (*She studies medicine.*)
c To jest mój ojciec.
  (*Pleased to meet you.*)
d Czy to jest zły pies?
  (*No, it's a good dog.*)

Did you know?
Nobel Prizes have been won seven times by six different Poles:

▶ 1903 – Maria Skłodowska-Curie – Physics
▶ 1905 – Henryk Sienkiewicz – Literature
▶ 1911 – Maria Skłodowska-Curie – Chemistry
▶ 1924 – Władysław Reymont – Literature
▶ 1980 – Czesław Miłosz – Literature
▶ 1983 – Lech Wałęsa – Peace
▶ 1996 – Wisława Szymborska – Literature

Insight

Another way of expanding your Polish learning game is to include a set of purple cards which contain general knowledge questions (in English). An information section, such as the one above, can be a good source for the questions, for example:

1 How many Poles have won the Nobel Prize?
2 How many times have Poles won the Nobel Prize?
3 In what categories have Poles won the Nobel Prize?
4 Who and in what year was the last Polish winner?

In this way you can build your own collection of Polish trivia.

3

Jestem szczęśliwy – mam czas i pieniądze
I'm happy – I've got time and money

In this unit you will learn
- *how to say you have or haven't got something*
- *how to ask if somebody has something*
- *how to say you have got time to do something*

In Units 1 and 2 you met the important verb **być** which allows you to express who you are and introduce or describe yourself and others. In this unit you will learn how to express what you have and ask what others possess.

Dialogue 1 **Dialog pierwszy**

Andrew and Maria are talking about Andrew's family in Poland.

Vocabulary **Słówka**

Form in the dialogue	Dictionary form	English translation
ma	mieć	*(s/he/it) has*
w + locative*		*(located) in*

w Polsce	Polska	*in Poland*
chyba		*I think, I suppose*
problem		*problem*
jaki		*what (sort of)*
ani … ani …		*neither … nor …*
adresu	adres	*address*
nazwiska	nazwisko	*surname*
żaden		*none*
To żaden problem.		*It's no problem at all.*
kontakty	kontakt	*contacts*
archiwum (neuter)		*archive(s)*

*This is explained in the Grammar appendix.

Maria	Czy ma pan rodzinę w Polsce?	*Have you got any family in Poland?*
Andrew	Chyba tak, ale mam problem.	*I think so, but I have a problem.*
Maria	Jaki problem?	*What sort of problem?*
Andrew	Nie mam ani nazwiska, ani adresu.	*I haven't got either a surname or an address.*
Maria	To żaden problem. Mam kontakty w Archiwum.	*It's no problem at all. I've got some contacts at the Archive.*

How the language works

Żaden is an interesting word; it means *no, not a single, not any, none at all*. It's frequently used in colloquial Polish and is best learned through phrases such as the one used by Maria in the previous dialogue. Here are some more examples:

za żadne pieniądze/skarby	*no way, not for all the tea in China* (or literally: *for no money/treasures*)
Jan nie ma żadnych przyjaciół.	*John has no friends at all.*
pod żadnym pozorem	*under no circumstances* (or lit.: *under no appearance*)

Dialogue 2 **Dialog drugi**

Maria needs to get together some more information about Andrew's family. She asks if he's got time to stay a bit longer and have another cup of tea.

Vocabulary **Słówka**

Form in the dialogue	Dictionary form	English translation
czas na + acc.		*time for*
herbatę	herbata	*tea*
dużo		*a lot*
rodzinne	rodzinny	*family* (adj.)
dokumenty	dokument	*documents*
fotografie	fotografia	*photographs*

Maria	Czy ma pan jeszcze czas na herbatę?	*Have you still got time for (a cup of) tea?*
Andrew	Tak, mam dużo czasu.	*Yes, I have plenty of time.*
Maria	Czy ma pan jakieś rodzinne dokumenty?	*Have you got any family documents?*

| Andrew | Tak, mam. Proszę, to są dokumenty i fotografie. | *Yes, I have. Here you are, these are the documents and photographs.* |
| Maria | Dziękuję. | *Thank you.* |

Dialogue 3 **Dialog trzeci**

While Maria is looking through Andrew's documents, he asks her about her family.

Vocabulary **Słówka**

Form in the dialogue	Dictionary form	English translation
męża	mąż	*husband*
syna	syn	*son*
architektem	architekt	*architect*
dobrą pracę	dobra, praca	*a good job*
pieniądze (plural)		*money*
rodziny	rodzina	*family*
dzieci	dziecko	*children*
imię		*first name, Christian name*
na emeryturze	na, emerytura	*on a pension, retired*

Andrew	Czy pani ma rodzinę?	*Have you got any family?*
Maria	Tak, mam, męża i syna. To jest mój syn. Jest architektem. Ma dobrą pracę i pieniądze, ale nie ma dzieci.	*Yes, I have, a husband and a son. This is my son. He's an architect. He's got a good job and money, but he hasn't any family (children).*
Andrew	A pani mąż?	*And (what about) your husband?*
Maria	Mój mąż ma na imię Piotr. Też jest na emeryturze.	*My husband's name is Piotr. He's also retired.*

As in the previous units, listen to the dialogues as many times as
you need until you feel confident.

Start building your own word collection. It's a great way of learning new
words and phrases. The best way to do it is by using index cards stored in
an index box and arranged alphabetically.

You can allocate different colours to different categories, for example:

▶ nouns – navy blue
▶ adjectives – light blue
▶ verbs – red
▶ adverbs – pink.

Cards should be big enough to contain basic information on the front
and additional details on the back. See an example below:

> Word: **detektyw**
> English translation: *detective*
> Gender: masculine
> Examples: **Jestem detektywem.**

The more you learn, the more information you can add to the card such as:

▶ different examples
▶ what the word looks like for different cases
▶ what the plural form is, etc.

You can add new words or expand the information on words you
already know.

Let's practise

▶ Copy the dialogues (both Polish and English parts) onto small
pieces of paper.

- ▶ Mix the pieces and reconstruct the dialogues correctly (both parts).
- ▶ Mix the pieces again and reconstruct the Polish side of the dialogues.

◀) **CD1, TR 20**

Listen and repeat

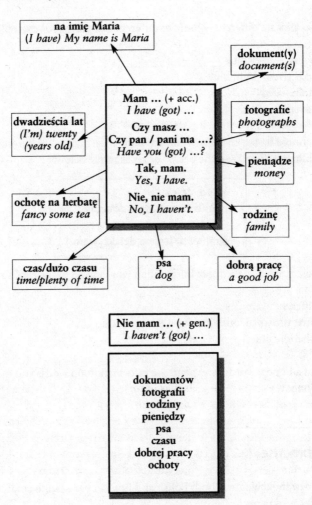

na imię Maria
(I have) My name is Maria

dokument(y)
document(s)

fotografie
photographs

dwadzieścia lat
*(I'm) twenty
(years old)*

Mam … (+ acc.)
I have (got) …

**Czy masz …
Czy pan / pani ma …?**
Have you (got) …?

Tak, mam.
Yes, I have.

Nie, nie mam.
No, I haven't.

pieniądze
money

ochotę na herbatę
fancy some tea

rodzinę
family

czas/dużo czasu
time/plenty of time

psa
dog

dobrą pracę
a good job

Nie mam … (+ gen.)
I haven't (got) …

dokumentów
fotografii
rodziny
pieniędzy
psa
czasu
dobrej pracy
ochoty

- ▶ Separate the Polish and English parts of the dialogues. Turn the Polish parts face down and mix them again. Turn them face up at random and translate into English.
- ▶ Do the same exercise with the English part of the dialogues.
- ▶ Arrange the Polish side of the dialogue in the correct order, turn Andrew's part face down and try to speak his part without looking.
- ▶ Repeat the same exercises with Maria's part.

◀) CD1, TR 21

Pronunciation guide Jak to wymówić?

Consonants (part 1) – soft consonants

Any letter that does not represent a vowel (a, ą, e, ę, i, o, ó, u, y) represents a consonant. The following are all consonants:

b, c, ć, d, f, g, h, j, k, l, ł, m, n, ń, p, r, s, ś, t, w, z, ź, ż

We've already mentioned that the following are produced much the same way as in English:

b, d, f, g, k, l, m, n, p, s, t, z

So what's left is:

c, ć, g, h, j, ł, ń, r, ś, w, ż, ź

The letter **c** normally represents *ts* as in *cats*. Its name is [tse] (like English *outset* but without the *ou* and the final *t*), which we can represent the Polish way: [ce]. English ears perceive this *ts* as two sounds, but for Poles it's a single sound, as in the middle of the name **Jacek** (ja-tsek). The name of the letter [ce] reflects the way the letter is pronounced unless it comes before **h, i** or **z**. These three combinations – **ch, ci** and **cz** – will be covered separately.

The letter **j** normally represent the same sound as the *y* in English *yes*.

The letter **ł** now normally represents a sound like the English *w*; most Poles now pronounce it like the *w* in English *mower*. This letter does not have a strong sound, and you may well get the impression it has disappeared when someone speaking fast pronounces **chciała** as [chciaa].

The letter **r** represents a rolled (trilled) *r*, as in Russian or Spanish or old-fashioned stereotypical Scots English. If you're unable to make this sound, be aware that a few Poles pronounce it like a French *r*, so you have this to fall back on.

The letter **w** represents the same sound as an English *v*.

All consonants are divided into two groups: hard and soft consonants. So how do you know which is which? The clue to a soft consonant is the accent above the letter, so the following letters are soft consonants: **ć, ń, ś, ź.**

- ▶ **ć** is like *ch* in *cheap*
- ▶ **ń** is like the first *n(i)* in *union*
- ▶ **ś** is like *sh* in *sheep*
- ▶ **ź** is like *s* in *please yourself* (said quickly).

Listen and repeat

ćma	*moth*
koń	*horse*
środek	*middle/centre*
źródło	*spring/source*

How the language works

Introductions

Talking about her husband, Maria says **Mój mąż ma na imię Piotr** *My husband's name is Piotr*, thus demonstrating the second way of introducing yourself or someone else if you are using just the first name:

I	Mam na imię James.	*My (first) name's James.*
you	Jak masz na imię?	*What's your first name?*
he	Ma na imię Stefan.	*His name's Stefan.*
she	Ma na imię Barbara.	*Her name's Barbara.*
you, polite	Pan ma na imię Robert?	*Is your first name Robert?*
	Pani ma na imię Anna?	*Is your first name Anna?*

'Jestem emerytem/emerytką' *I'm retired* vs. 'Jestem na emeryturze' (lit.: *I'm on a retirement pension*)

In Polish there are two ways of saying you're retired:

Jestem emerytem/emerytką.	*I'm a retired (man/woman).*
Jestem na emeryturze.	*(lit.) I'm on a (retirement) pension.*

If you've been retired for health reasons and you are entitled to a special health or medical pension, you say:

Jestem rencistą/rencistką.	*I'm a retired (man/woman).*
Jestem na rencie.	

Mieć in Polish is used in similar contexts as in English to express possession:

Mam czas.	*I have time.*
Mam samochód.	*I have a car.*
Mam rodzinę.	*I have a family.*

Unlike in English, however, it is also used to describe how old people are and to express what you fancy:

Mam dwadzieścia lat.	*I am twenty (years old).*
On ma trzydzieści lat.	*He is thirty (years old).*
Maria ma sześćdziesiąt pięć lat.	*Maria is sixty-five (years old).*
Mam ochotę na herbatę.	*I fancy some tea.*
Maria ma ochotę na spacer.	*Maria fancies a walk.*

The haves and the have nots

The verb **mieć** *to have* looks like this in the present tense:

(ja)	mam	*I have*	Mam rodzinę. *I have a family.*
(ty)	masz	*you (familiar, to one person) have*	Masz rodzinę. *You have a family.*
(on, ona, ono); pan, pani	ma	*s/he/it has; you (polite m./f.) have*	On/ona/ono ma rodzinę. *S/he/it/ madam/sir has a family.*
(my)	mamy	*we have*	Mamy rodzinę. *We have a family.*
(wy)	macie	*you (familiar) have*	Macie rodzinę. *You have a family.*
(oni, one), panowie, panie, państwo	mają	*they, gentlemen, ladies, ladies and gentlemen, have*	Oni/one/panie/ panowie państwo mają rodzinę. *They have a family.*

More about having – the accusative or how to be affirmative

Forms of **mieć** are completed or complemented by a 'direct object'. In Polish you can't just have, you have to have 'something'. The something (or direct object) will be in the accusative case; that's the traditional term for it.

Let's have a look at some examples from the course so far:

Subject	Verb	Direct object	
[Ja]	Mam	dokument.	*I've got a document.*
Andrew	ma	czas.	*Andrew has got time.*
Maria	ma	rodzinne fotografie.	*Maria has family photographs.*

These sentences are examples of the affirmative accusative rule since they are affirmative (they are not negative or questions) and we used the accusative form.

We will return to discuss accusative forms in Unit 6.

To have not! – the negative genitive rule

But why does it matter if the sentence is affirmative or negative? It matters because when you negate a verb like **mieć** in Polish, the direct object complementing it changes from the accusative to the genitive form:

Affirmative accusative form	Negative genitive form
Mam dokument. *(I have a document.)*	Nie mam dokumentu. *(I haven't a document.)*
Andrew ma czas. *(Andrew has time.)*	Andrew nie ma czasu. *(Andrew hasn't time.)*
Mam rodzinne fotografie. *(I have family photos.)*	Nie mam rodzinnych fotografii. *(I haven't family photos.)*

Insight

Some of my students benefit from imagining the verb **mieć** *to have* as a traveller who cannot travel alone – who must have a companion, either a happy, positive accusative or a grumpy, negative genitive.

So how do I create a genitive form?

Masculine nouns ending in a consonant typically add **-u** or **-a**:

Nominative		Accusative	Genitive
dokument	*(document)*	dokument	dokumentu
czas	*(time)*	czas	czasu
detektyw	*(detective)*	detektywa	detektywa
kot	*(cat)*	kota	kota

You'll have noticed from the examples above that sometimes the nominative and accusative look identical and sometimes the accusative and genitive look identical. So what's the rule?

▶ For animate masculine nouns (person, an animal or a living thing e.g. **detektyw/kot:**) genitive = accusative.
▶ For inanimate masculine nouns (objects, things that are not alive e.g. **dokument/czas**) nominative = accusative.

Feminine nouns typically change from -**a** to -**y**. Those which end -**ga** and -**ka** change to -**gi** and -**ki**.

Nominative		Accusative	Genitive
żona	(wife)	żonę	żony
rodzina	(family)	rodzinę	rodziny
fotografia	(photo)	fotografię	fotografii
córka	(daughter)	córkę	córki
książka	(book)	książkę	książki

Neuter nouns look much like masculine nouns with the genitive in -**a** instead of the -**o** or -**e**.

Nominative		Accusative	Genitive
dziecko	(child)	dziecko	dziecka
piwo	(beer)	piwo	piwa
wino	(wine)	wino	wina
mleko	(milk)	mleko	mleka

Pronunciation guide **Jak to wymówić?**

Consonants (part 2) – hard consonants

In Polish there are 16 hard consonants:

b, c, d, f, g, h, k, l, m, n, p, r, s, t, z, ż

Listen and repeat

Let's practise them by listening and repeating the following words out loud:

dobry	*good*	kto	*who*	klasa	*class/ classroom*
pani	*lady*	to	*this, it*	gazeta	*newspaper*
pan	*gentleman*	medycyna	*medicine*	dokument	*document*
bardzo	*very*	studentka	*female student*	fotografia	*photograph*
proszę	*please*	córka	*daughter*	żaden	*no, none*
wejść	*come in*	żona	*wife*	kontakty	*contacts*
trochę	*a bit*	mama	*Mum*	problem	*problem*
zmęczony	*tired*	brat	*brother*	archiwum	*archive*
głodny	*hungry*	herbata	*tea*	kawa	*coffee*

Test yourself

Exercise 1

Translate the following sentences into Polish and as usual check your answers and pronunciation by using the recording. Don't be shy: say your answers out loud! If you want to add new cards to your language game, the following sentences belong to the translation category (blue cards).

a I've got family in Poland.
b I've got a problem.
c I fancy some tea.
d Have you got any contacts at the Archives?
e I haven't got time.
f I've plenty of time.
g Have you got any documents? (to a woman)
h My daughter has a good job.
i I have a dog, Rex.
j I'm 20 (years old).

◆) **CD1, TR 24**

Exercise 2

Respond in Polish to the following statements and questions. Again, check your answers and pronunciation for both questions and answers on the recording. This is a communication exercise so you can add the questions to the yellow category of cards.

a Czy ma pan rodzinę w Polsce?
(I think so.)
b Mam problem.
(What sort of problem?)
c Czy ma pani czas na herbatę?
(Yes, I've got lots of time.)
d Czy ma pan ochotę na herbatę?
(Yes I have.)

Exercise 3

Turn the affirmative sentences into negative ones. Please remember to make all the necessary changes where appropriate. This exercise tests your grammatical skills so you can add them to the green category of cards.

a Mam czas.
b Mam rodzinę.
c Mam dobrą pracę.
d Mój syn jest architektem.

e Mam pieniądze.
f Andrew ma dokumenty i fotografię.
g Mają psa.
h To jest mój ojciec.
i Ona jest bardzo ładna.

Exercise 4

The following sentences give the answer to a question. What would be the question? This is another communication exercise so you may want to add it to the yellow category.

Example:

A: Tak, mam czas na herbatę.
Q: Czy masz/ma pan/pani czas na herbatę?

a Jestem emerytką.
b To jest mój ojciec.
c Nie, to nie jest mój ojciec. To jest mój dziadek.
d Tak, mam dokumenty.
e Nie, Azor to dobry pies.

Did you know?
▶ Poland was one of the first countries which officially recognized the importance of education for all children. In 1773, the Polish Parliament founded the Education Commission (Komisja Edukacyjna), the first Ministry of Education in the world.
▶ Two years later in 1775, the Parliament founded the Hospital Commission (Komisja Szpitalna) – the first Ministry of Health in the world. Its task was to oversee hospitals, charities, health and welfare.
▶ Poland was the first country in Europe (and second in the world after the United States) to adopt a written constitution. The Polish Parliament adopted it on 3 May 1791 and it was called the 3 May Constitution.

Insight
You can turn the facts above into a selection of general knowledge category questions (purple cards).

Muszę już iść
I've got to go now

In this unit you will learn
- *how to say you must/have to do something*
- *how to say you don't have to do something*
- *how to tell the time*

There are many situations in everyday life when we need to express what we must do and in this unit you will learn how to do this in Polish.

Dialogue 1 **Dialog pierwszy**

Andrew looks at his watch. He realizes it has stopped and that he must have spent a few hours with Maria. He still has a lot of things to sort out and has to go now.

Vocabulary **Słówka**

Form in the dialogue	Dictionary form	English translation
przepraszam	przepraszać > przeprosić	*sorry, excuse me, I apologize*
która godzina?	który, godzina	*what's the time (which hour?)*
czwarta	czwarty	*four o'clock (the fourth hour)*
niestety		*unfortunately, sadly*

muszę	musieć	*I must/I have to*
już		*already, now*
iść		*to go*
muszę już iść		*I must go now/I have to go now*
ojej		*oh dear*
szkoda		*pity, waste*

Andrew	Przepraszam, która godzina?	*Excuse me, what's the time?*
Maria	Czwarta.	*It's four o'clock.*
Andrew	Niestety, muszę już iść.	*Unfortunately, I have to go.*
Maria	Ojej, szkoda.	*Oh dear, that's a pity.*

◄» **CD1, TR 26**

Telling the time

To say what the time is, Poles use 'the ... th hour':

Listen and repeat

1:00	(Jest) (godzina) pierwsza.	*(It's) one (o'clock).*
		'It's the first hour.'
2:00	(Jest) (godzina) druga.	*(It's) two (o'clock).*
		'It's the second hour.'
3:00	(Jest) (godzina) trzecia.	*(It's) three (o'clock).*
		'It's the third hour.'
4:00	(Jest) (godzina) czwarta.	*(It's) four (o'clock).*
		'It's the fourth hour.'
5:00	(Jest) (godzina) piąta.	*(It's) five (o'clock).*
		'It's the fifth hour.'
6:00	(Jest) (godzina) szósta.	*(It's) six (o'clock).*
		'It's the sixth hour.'
7:00	(Jest) (godzina) siódma.	*(It's) seven (o'clock).*
		'It's the seventh hour.'
8:00	(Jest) (godzina) ósma.	*(It's) eight (o'clock).*
		'It's the eighth hour.'

9:00	(Jest) (godzina) dziewiąta.	*(It's) nine (o'clock).*
		'It's the ninth hour.'
10:00	(Jest) (godzina) dziesiąta.	*(It's) ten (o'clock).*
		'It's the tenth hour.'
11:00	(Jest) (godzina) jedenasta.	*(It's) eleven (o'clock).*
		'It's the eleventh hour.'
12:00	(Jest) (godzina) dwunasta.	*(It's) twelve (o'clock).* '
		It's the twelfth hour.'

To say *It's one o'clock*, it's usually sufficient to just say **Pierwsza**. However, it's also perfectly correct to use any of the following forms:

Godzina pierwsza.
Jest godzina pierwsza.
Jest pierwsza.

Dialogue 2 **Dialog drugi**

Andrew tries to explain what he still has to do.

Vocabulary **Słówka**

Form in the dialogue	Dictionary form	English translation
dlaczego		*why*
musi pan		*you must*
wrócić do + gen.	wracać > wrócić	*come/go back to*
załatwić	załatwiać > załatwić	*deal with, do, settle*
kilka		*a few, several*
spraw	sprawa	*thing, matter, problem*
wymienić	wymieniać > wymienić	*change, exchange, enumerate*
pieniądze (plural)		*money*
zadzwonić	dzwonić > zadzwonić	*ring, telephone*
do		*to*
domu	dom	*home, house*
hotelu	hotel	*hotel*
rozpakować się	rozpakowywać się > rozpakować się	*get unpacked*
potem		*then, next, afterwards*

Maria	Dlaczego musi pan iść?	*Why do you have to go?*
Andrew	Muszę załatwić kilka spraw.	*I have to sort out a few things.*
	Muszę wrócić do hotelu i rozpakować się.	*I have to return to the hotel and unpack.*
	Potem muszę wymienić pieniądze i zadzwonić do domu.	*Then I have to exchange some money and phone home.*

Dialogue 3 **Dialog trzeci**

Maria can think of at least two more things that Andrew has to do.

Vocabulary **Słówka**

Form in the dialogue	Dictionary form	English translation
zwiedzić	zwiedzać > zwiedzić	*visit, go sightseeing in*
koniecznie		*necessarily, absolutely (must)*
spotkać się	spotykać się > spotkać się	*meet, get together*
znowu		*again*
bardzo chętnie		*very happily, willingly, would love to*

Maria	Musi pan też zwiedzić Kraków.	*You also have to (sight) see Kraków.*
Andrew	O tak, koniecznie.	*Oh yes, absolutely.*
Maria	Musimy spotkać się znowu.	*We have to meet again.*
Andrew	Tak. Bardzo chętnie.	*Yes, I'd love to.*

Insight

Although it is important to make sure you listen to the dialogues several times and you feel confident that you understand them, don't be too hard on yourself if the text seems too difficult. Leave it and go back to the previous dialogues. Hopefully they will seem so much easier. After a while return to the dialogue which you struggled with initially – I'm sure it will seem easier second time round.

Let's practise

▶ Copy the dialogues (both Polish and English parts) onto small pieces of paper.
▶ Mix the pieces and reconstruct the dialogues correctly (both parts).
▶ Mix the pieces again and reconstruct the Polish side of the dialogues.
▶ Separate the Polish and English parts of the dialogues. Turn the Polish parts face down and mix them again. Turn them face up at random and translate into English.
▶ Do the same exercise with the English part of the dialogues.
▶ Arrange the Polish side of the dialogue in the correct order, turn Andrew's part face down and try to speak his part without looking.
▶ Repeat the same exercises with Maria's part.

◀) **CD1, TR 30**

Pronunciation guide Jak to wymówić?

The double life of 'i' or how to turn a hard consonant into a soft one

There is more to the vowel **i** than meets the eye. For example, the nouns **pani**, **archiwum** and **fotografia** all have a hard consonant (**n** in pani, **h** in archiwum and (second) **f** in fotografia) which is followed by **i**. This particular combination means that a hard consonant is no longer hard; it become soft just like the consonants with an accent.

If any of the soft consonants are followed by a vowel then an accent is replaced by **i**. However, the pronunciation stays the same.

Practise by listening to and repeating the following words out loud:

ciało	*body*	dzień	*day*
niebo	*sky*	dziki	*wild*

cierpieć	*to suffer*	sień	*hallway*
ziarno	*grain*	łokieć	*elbow*
widzieć	*to see*	cień	*shadow*
miska	*bowl*	pisklę	*chick*
dni	*days*	list	*letter*
biały	*white*	wiotki	*limp*

How the language works

The verb 'musieć'

Unlike English, with its choice of *must* and *have to*, Polish just has the verb **musieć**. The good news is that verbs following **musieć** are always in their infinitive form. An infinitive is the form of a verb that corresponds to the basic one that follows *to* in English; indeed a lot of people like to include the *to* when quoting English infinitives: *He refused to budge.* *She likes to swim. It tends to go wrong. To be or not to be?* An oddity of English is that *must*, unlike Polish **musieć**, has no infinitive of its own and has to borrow from *have to*; we can't say *I wouldn't like to must do that*, but instead we have to say, *I wouldn't like to have to do that.*

This is how **musieć** is used in all persons:

I	ja	muszę	Muszę zobaczyć Kraków.
			I must see Kraków.
you	ty	musisz	Musisz zobaczyć Kraków.
			You must see Kraków.
s/he/it	on/ona/ ono	musi	On/ona/ono musi zobaczyć Kraków.
			S/he/it must see Kraków.
	pan/pani	musi	Pan/pani musi zobaczyć Kraków.
			Sir/madam must see Kraków.
we	my	musimy	Musimy zobaczyć Kraków.
			We must see Kraków.
you (group)	wy	musicie	Musicie zobaczyć Kraków.
			You must see Kraków.

they	oni, one	muszą	Oni/one muszą zobaczyć Kraków. *They have to see Kraków.*
	panowie, panie	muszą	Panowie/Panie muszą zobaczyć Kraków. *Ladies/gentlemen must see Kraków.*
	państwo	muszą	Państwo muszą zobaczyć Kraków. *Ladies and gentlemen must see Kraków.*

Mustn't and *don't have to* ...

Note that in English *you mustn't* means that you are not allowed to, whereas in Polish **nie musisz** means *you don't have to.*

Nie musisz jechać do Krakowa.	*You don't have to go to Kraków.*
Nie musisz pić piwa.	*You don't have to drink beer.*
Nie muszę, ale chcę.	*I don't have to, but I want to.*

Things we do (to) ourselves/each other – reflexive verbs

Musimy spotkać się znowu.	*We must meet (each other) again.*

In the example above you can see that in English it's enough to say we must meet again. Polish is more precise here, and makes it clear that it's each other we must meet, not just anybody. The Polish verb here is reflexive, indicating that people are planning to do something to themselves or each other. It's easy to recognize a reflexive verb because it has **się** attached to it. Polish uses the same **się** for *myself, yourself, himself, herself, itself, ourselves, yourself* and *themselves*:

Spotykam się z bratem.	*I meet my brother. (I meet myself with my brother.)*
Spotykasz się z bratem.	*You meet your brother.*
Spotyka się z bratem.	*S/he meets her/his brother.*
Spotykamy się z bratem.	*We meet our brother.*
Spotykacie się z bratem.	*You meet your brother.*
Spotykają się z bratem.	*They meet their brother.*

Similarly, **się** is used with the **pan**-words in the polite form of address:

Jak często pan(i) się spotyka z bratem?
How often do you meet your brother?

Jak często panie/panowie/ państwo się spotykają?
How often do you meet up?

Polish is generally more explicit than English about the fact you are doing something to yourself:

Myję się.
I'm washing (myself).

Golę się.
I'm shaving (myself).

But Polish can sometimes be quite loose about what counts as doing something to yourself:

pakować się
to pack (your things or your bags, rather than yourself)

rozpakować się
to unpack (your things or your bags, rather than yourself)

It's worth remembering that not all Polish reflexive verbs have their reflexive counterparts in English.

It is also worth remembering that się can follow and proceed as well as get separated from the verb it refers to. For example:

Musimy spotkać się znowu.
Musimy się spotkać znowu.
Musimy się znowu spotkać.

The change of order is dictated by the rhythm of the sentence, and it does not alter the meaning.

◆) CD1, TR 31

Listen and repeat

The following diagrams give you examples from the dialogues, as well as more practical examples not used in the text but common in everyday Polish.

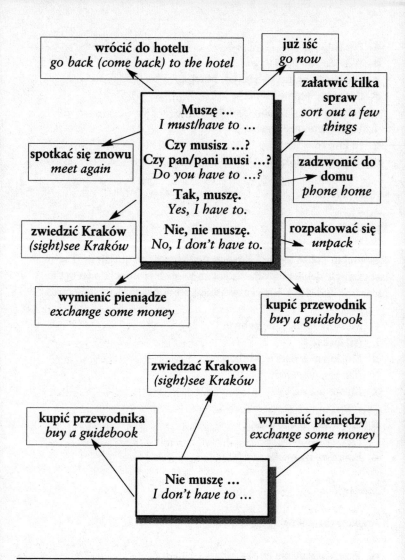

wrócić do hotelu
go back (come back) to the hotel

już iść
go now

załatwić kilka spraw
sort out a few things

Muszę ...
I must/have to ...

Czy musisz ...?
Czy pan/pani musi ...?
Do you have to ...?

Tak, muszę.
Yes, I have to.

Nie, nie muszę.
No, I don't have to.

spotkać się znowu
meet again

zadzwonić do domu
phone home

zwiedzić Kraków
(sight)see Kraków

rozpakować się
unpack

wymienić pieniądze
exchange some money

kupić przewodnik
buy a guidebook

zwiedzać Krakowa
(sight)see Kraków

kupić przewodnika
buy a guidebook

wymienić pieniędzy
exchange some money

Nie muszę ...
I don't have to ...

Test yourself

Exercise 1

Translate the following sentences into Polish. Remember to say the sentences out loud! (blue (translation) cards)

a I've got to go.
b Why do you have to go?
c She has to return to her (**jej**) hotel.
d I've got to phone home.
e You must see London (**Londyn**).
f We have to meet again.
g I'd love to.
h Oh yes, absolutely.

◀)) CD1, TR 32

Exercise 2

Respond in Polish to the following statements and questions. The last example deliberately hasn't got an English prompt. Listen to the recording and check your answers and pronunciation. (yellow cards)

a Musimy spotkać się znowu.
  (*I'd love to.*)
b Musi pani zwiedzić Kraków.
  (*Oh yes, absolutely.*)
c Muszę już iść.
  (*Pity.*)
d Czy masz trochę czasu?
  (*Yes, I have.*)
e Poproszę nazwisko.

Exercise 3

Complete the following sentences.

a Przepraszam, ale muszę już _____.
b Andrew musi rozpakować _____.
c Ewa musi wymienić _____.
d Musi pan _____ Kraków.
e Tomek musi załatwić kilka _____.

Did you know?

▶ Poles like spending their free time outdoors. Hill walking, mountaineering, skiing and sailing are some of the most popular sports for Poles. For less sporty types, allotments (**działki**) are a popular way of spending time away from towns and cities.

▶ A lot of Poles like nothing more than to spend many an idle hour fishing. Angling (**wędkarstwo**) is a very popular pastime.

▶ Another favourite pastime of many Poles, especially of the older generation, is wild mushroom picking. Considering that a third of the Polish countryside is covered in forest, this is not surprising. In fact, all fruits of the forest such as blueberries and wild strawberries are held in high esteem.

5

Chciał(a)bym zamówić stolik
I'd like to book a table

In this unit you will learn
- *how to say you would or wouldn't like to do something*
- *how to ask how someone is*
- *how to ask for help and information*
- *how to say numbers 0–100*

Chciał(a)bym *I would like* is one of the most useful polite phrases in everyday Polish. You'll hear it everywhere and have plenty of opportunity to practise it as well. It has two versions: **chciałbym** if you're male, and **chciałabym** if you're female.

Dialogue 1 **Dialog pierwszy**

Andrew is leaving Maria's apartment. Once again, he expresses his desire to track down his relatives.

Vocabulary **Słówka**

Form in the dialogue	Dictionary form	English translation
spotkanie		*meeting, get together*
nie ma za co		*don't mention it, you're welcome, my pleasure,*

		there isn't anything (to thank) for, not at all
dziękuję za znaleźć	dziękować > podziękować	thank you for
	znajdować > znaleźć	find
do zobaczenia	zobaczenie; widzieć > zobaczyć	see you
jutro		tomorrow

CD1. TR 33

Andrew	Dziękuję za spotkanie.	*Thank you for the meeting.*
Maria	Nie ma za co.	*You're welcome/not at all.*
Andrew	Tak bardzo chciałbym znaleźć moją rodzinę.	*I would so like to find my family.*
Maria	Oczywiście, rozumiem. Do zobaczenia jutro.	*Of course, I understand. See you tomorrow.*

Dialogue 2 Dialog drugi

Andrew goes back to his hotel. He has unpacked his things and now he feels hungry. He phones the reception desk and books a table in the hotel restaurant.

Vocabulary Słówka

Form in the dialogue	Dictionary form	English translation
dzień dobry	dzień, dobry	*hello, good morning, good afternoon*
restauracja (f)		*restaurant*
słucham	słuchać	*listen (here: Can I help you?)*
zamówić	zamawiać > zamówić	*to order*
stolik (m)		*table in a restaurant, small table*
recepcja		*reception (desk)*

na którą godzinę	która godzina	*what time for, when for*
poproszę	prosić > poprosić	*please (extra polite)*
do widzenia	widzenie; widzieć >	*goodbye (till we see*
	zobaczyć	*each other)*
pokój		*room*

Receptionist	Dzień dobry, recepcja. Słucham.	*Good afternoon, reception. Can I help?*
Andrew	Dzień dobry. Chciałbym zamówić stolik w restauracji.	*Good afternoon. I'd like to book a table in the restaurant.*
Receptionist	Na którą godzinę?	*(For) what time?*
Andrew	Na siódmą trzydzieści.	*For seven thirty.*
Receptionist	Poproszę nazwisko.	*Can I have your name, please?*
Andrew	Stewart.	*Stewart.*
Receptionist	Pan Andrew Stewart?	*Mr Andrew Stewart?*
Andrew	Tak.	*Yes.*
Receptionist	Pokój sto dwadzieścia pięć?	*Room 125?*
Andrew	Tak.	*Yes.*
Receptionist	Proszę bardzo.	*Certainly.*
Andrew	Dziękuję bardzo. Do widzenia.	*Thank you very much. Bye.*

Dialogue 3 **Dialog trzeci**

Meanwhile, Maria telephones her friend, Ewa, who works in the
Archiwum Państwowe (*State Archives*) in Kraków. Maria needs Ewa's
help to trace Andrew's family in Poland.

Vocabulary **Słówka**

Form in the dialogue	Dictionary form	English translation
słucham	słuchać	hello, I'm listening, pardon?, can I help you?
mówi	mówić > powiedzieć	is speaking, speaks
cześć		hi
słychać + acc.		... can be heard
co słychać?		how are things? what's new?
z + instrumental		with
z tobą	ty	with you
potrzebuję pomocy	potrzebować + gen., pomoc	I need help
zasięgnąć informacji	zasięgać > zasięgnąć, informacje (pl.)	get some information
dokumenty	dokument	documents
dobrze	dobry	OK, correctly, well, right

Ewa	Słucham.	*Hello.*
Maria	Cześć. Mówi Maria.	*Hi. Maria speaking.*
Ewa	Cześć. Co słychać?	*Hi. How are you?*
Maria	Dziękuję, dobrze.	*Fine, thanks.*
	Chciałabym spotkać się z tobą.	*I'd like to meet up with you.*
	Potrzebuję pomocy.	*I need some help.*
Ewa	Jakiej pomocy?	*What sort of help?*

◆ CD1, TR 35

| Maria | Chciałabym zasięgnąć informacji i znaleźć dokumenty. | I'd like to get some information and to find some documents. |
| Ewa | Dobrze. | OK. |

Let's practise

▶ Copy the dialogues (both Polish and English parts) onto small pieces of paper.

▶ Mix the pieces and reconstruct the dialogues correctly (both parts).

▶ Mix the pieces again and reconstruct the Polish side of the dialogues.

▶ Separate the Polish and English parts of the dialogues. Turn the Polish parts face down and mix them again. Turn them face up at random and translate into English.

▶ Do the same exercise with the English part of the dialogues.

▶ Arrange the Polish side of the dialogue in the correct order, turn Andrew's/Ewa's part face down and try to speak their parts without looking.

▶ Repeat the same exercises with Maria's part.

How the language works

'I would like' and 'I must/have to'

Because **chciał(a)bym** *I would like* and **muszę** *I must/have to* behave grammatically in the same way when used with other verbs, you can easily substitute one for the other in all the examples you have seen in this and in the previous unit:

Chciał(a)bym już iść.	*I'd like to go now.*
Muszę już iść.	*I have to go now.*
Chciał(a)bym zamówić taksówkę.	*I'd like to book a taxi.*
Muszę zamówić taksówkę.	*I have to book a taxi.*
Chciał(a)bym wymienić pieniądze.	*I'd like to exchange some money.*
Muszę wymienić pieniądze.	*I have to exchange some money.*

| Chciał(a)bym zrobić zakupy. | *I'd like to do some shopping.* |
| Muszę zrobić zakupy. | *I have to do some shopping.* |

So far you have met the first person singular form (*I*) of *would like* – **chciałbym** if you're male; **chciałabym** if you're female. Here are the remaining forms:

Singular		Masculine	Feminine
1st person	ja (*I*)	chciałbym	chciałabym
2nd person	ty (*you*)	chciałbyś	chciałabyś
3rd person	on (*he*)	chciałby	
	ona (*she*)		chciałaby
	pan (*you*)	chciałby	
	/pani		chciałaby

Plural		Virile	Non-virile (see next section)
1st person	my (*we*)	chcielibyśmy	chciałybyśmy
2nd person	wy (*you*)	chcielibyście	chciałybyście
3rd person	oni (*they, including masculine*)	chcieliby	
	one (*they, no masculine*)		chciałyby
	państwo (*you ladies and gentleman*), panowie (*you gentlemen*)	chcieliby	
	panie (*you ladies*)		chciałyby

The first person (*I*, *we*) is or includes the person speaking. The second person (*you*, one or more people) is the addressee, the person being spoken to, and the third person is any third party or entity not directly involved in the conversation: *he*, *she*, *it* (singular), *they* (plural).

As you know, and as the table shows, the third person singular and third person plural forms in Polish mean *they* unless a **pan**-word is attached to change them into a polite *you* (like the old-fashioned *Would madam like to try this on?* that used to be common in shops).

Look at the diagram on the opposite page. It will help you organize and practise more examples.

Not just men and women, but virile and non-virile

From the table on the previous page you can see that Polish lines up the genders differently in the singular and in the plural, something already hinted at when you met two words for *they*. The verb forms, too, are different, depending on whether you are talking about a group that includes grammatically masculine persons or a group that doesn't.

It's unfortunately quite common for textbooks to say simply that it's **oni** for men and **one** for women, and leave it at that. This isn't strictly true, though, attractively simple as it sounds. For one thing, it leaves out children, and for another, it overlooks mixed groups. Some examples will help to make this clear:

▶ **Chłopiec** *boy* and **syn** *son* are grammatically masculine, so **chłopcy** and **synowie**, their plurals, are virile. **Dziecko** *child*, on the other hand, is grammatically neuter, not masculine, so **nasze dzieci** *our children* are non-virile in the plural, even if all the children we're talking about are boys.

▶ If you refer to women (especially in large groups) as **wszyscy** *everybody*, or as **ludzie** *people*, even if no men are involved, then grammatically they're virile.

▶ If you think of men as **osoby** *persons*, which you're especially likely to do if you're counting them, then they're non-virile, because the word **osoba** *person* is grammatically feminine.

Don't worry, with further practice you will find that this concept will become easier to understand.

Chciał(a)bym vs. *nie chciał(a)bym*

As explained in Unit 3, grammatically speaking, nie used with Polish verbs changes the case for the direct object noun from the accusative to the genitive:

Subject	Verb	Direct object
(Ja)*	chciał(a)bym kupić	przewodnik. (acc.)
I	*would like to buy*	*a guide.*
(Ja)	nie chciał(a)bym kupić	przewodnika. (gen.)
I	*wouldn't like to buy*	*a guide.*
(Ja)	chciał(a)bym zwiedzić	Wawel. (acc.)
I	*would like to (sight)see*	*Wawel castle.*
(Ja)	nie chciał(a)bym zwiedzić	Wawelu. (gen.)
I	*wouldn't like to (sight)see*	*Wawel castle.*
(Ja)	chciał(a)bym zamówić	stolik. (acc.)
I	*would like to book*	*a table.*
(Ja)	nie chciał(a)bym zamówić	stolika. (gen.)
I	*wouldn't like to book*	*a table.*

*You don't need to include ja in the sentence because the ending of chciał(a)bym indicates that the first person singular is speaking.

This is a principle you will frequently come across in Polish. Furthermore, the case doesn't change if the accusative is not a direct object. For example, when negated, czekać na *to wait for* has to have an accusative with na and not a genitive.

(Nie) czekam na tramwaj.   *I'm (not) waiting for a tram.*

Sometimes the change of the case will be hidden by the fact that two cases coincide in form:

Mam psa.   *I've got a dog.*
Nie mam psa.   *I haven't got a dog.*

In the first example, **psa** is in the accusative case, which is like the genitive because the noun refers to a living being. Psa in the second example really is in the genitive case. The forms just look identical. Here are some more examples:

Nominative	Genitive	Accusative
pies (*dog*)	psa	psa
kot (*cat*)	kota	kota
koń (*horse*)	konia	konia
szczur (*rat*)	szczura	szczura

◀) **CD1, TR 36**

Listen and repeat

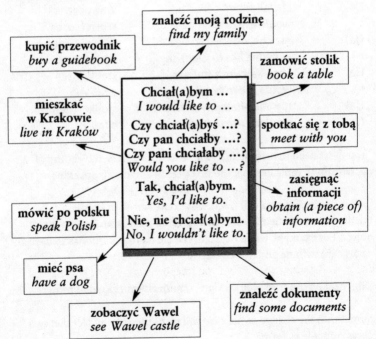

kupić przewodnik
buy a guidebook

znaleźć moją rodzinę
find my family

zamówić stolik
book a table

mieszkać
w Krakowie
live in Kraków

spotkać się z tobą
meet with you

Chciał(a)bym …
I would like to …

Czy chciał(a)byś …?
Czy pan chciałby …?
Czy pani chciałaby …?
Would you like to …?

Tak, chciał(a)bym.
Yes, I'd like to.

Nie, nie chciał(a)bym.
No, I wouldn't like to.

zasięgnąć
informacji
*obtain (a piece of)
information*

mówić po polsku
speak Polish

mieć psa
have a dog

zobaczyć Wawel
see Wawel castle

znaleźć dokumenty
find some documents

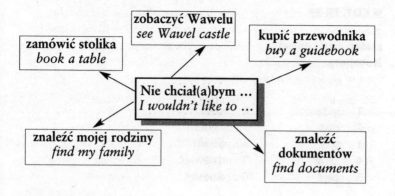

zamówić stolika
book a table

zobaczyć Wawelu
see Wawel castle

kupić przewodnika
buy a guidebook

Nie chciał(a)bym …
I wouldn't like to …

znaleźć mojej rodziny
find my family

znaleźć dokumentów
find documents

Insight

Word association is a great way to remember words and phrases.
You can do it in three ways:

▶ I can remember a Polish word because it looks like an English word.

   Kot looks like *cat*.
   Recepcja looks like *reception*.
   Restauracja looks like *restaurant*.

▶ I can remember a Polish word because it sounds like an English word.

   Park looks and sounds like *park* in English.

▶ I can remember a Polish word because I can create a story around it.

   pies (*dog*) – Can you imagine a dog eating a pie?
   brat (*brother*) – Can you imagine a naughty brother?

Listen and repeat
Numbers

First of all, let's learn to count up to ten.

1	jeden	6	sześć
2	dwa	7	siedem
3	trzy	8	osiem
4	cztery	9	dziewięć
5	pięć	10	dziesięć

Once you've got these numbers at your fingertips you can spell out any longer number digit by digit, provided you also know the word **zero** (0).

Now let's look at the numbers 11–19, all of which have a stressed **na** in them:

11	jedenaście
12	dwanaście
13	trzynaście
14	czternaście
15	piętnaście
16	szesnaście
17	siedemnaście
18	osiemnaście
19	dziewiętnaście

Now let's count up in tens:

20	dwadzieścia
30	trzydzieści
40	czterdzieści
50	pięćdziesiąt
60	sześćdziesiąt
70	siedemdziesiąt
80	osiemdziesiąt
90	dziewięćdziesiąt
100	sto

You can see how the basic numbers up to ten, 11–19, and the tens are related to each other. These words can be combined to describe other numbers (in-between and over 100), as you would expect:

24	dwadzieścia cztery
35	trzydzieści pięć
78	siedemdziesiąt osiem
89	osiemdziesiąt dziewięć
46	czterdzieści sześć
82	osiemdziesiąt dwa
93	dziewięćdziesiąt trzy
103	sto trzy
117	sto siedemnaście
155	sto pięćdziesiąt pięć
197	sto dziewięćdziesiąt siedem

You can practise your numbers by reading out loud telephone numbers, which Poles usually give in pairs of digits: **trzydzieści jeden zero dwa dwadzieścia siedem** (35-02-27), etc.

◆) **CD1, TR 38**

Pronunciation guide Jak to wymówić?

In Polish some consonants form permanent partnerships with other consonants which together represent one sound:

   ch, rz, sz, cz, dz, dż, dź

ch represents a single sound like the *ch* at the end of the Scots word *loch*. The letter **h** on its own is similarly pronounced. Don't be tempted to pronounce **ch** in any other way – in Polish it is always *ch* as in *loch*.

Listen and repeat

| chwila | *moment* |
| chętnie | *willingly* |

trochę	*a bit*
chyba	*perhaps*
archiwum	*archives*
architekt	*architect*
chciałbym	*I'd like to*
rachunek	*bill*
kuchnia	*kitchen/cuisine*
schody	*stairs*

Try these Polish words. Take them as slowly as you need to guarantee perfect smoothness, as that's the best road to long-term fluency:

czas	*time*	szkoła	*school*
deszcz	*rain*	szczur	*rat*
dżokej	*jockey*	trzeba	*one needs to*
żona	*wife*	ryż	*rice*

Unless followed by **i**, **dz** represents a single sound like the *ds* in *beds*, which to Poles is a single sound. Listen and repeat:

kukurydza	*maize*	sadza	*soot*

Test yourself

Exercise 1

Translate the following sentences into Polish. (blue cards)

a Thank you for the meeting.
b I'd like to find my family.
c I'd like to book a table.
d Can I have your name, please?
e How are you?
f (For) what time?
g For seven thirty.
h I'd like to meet you.
i I'd like to find some documents.

Exercise 2

Turn the affirmative sentences below into negative ones. (green cards)

a Chciałbym zamówić stolik.
b Chciałabym kupić przewodnik.
c Muszę zobaczyć Wawel.
d Mam konia.
e Chciałbym wymienić pieniądze.
f Muszę zrobić zakupy.
g Jestem głodny.

◆) **CD1, TR 39**

Exercise 3

Respond to the following English prompts. Check your answers and pronunciation on the recording. (yellow cards)

a Potrzebuję pomocy. *(What sort of help?)*
b Chciałbym zamówić taksówkę. *(Address, please.)*
c Czy jest pan Amerykaninem? (American) *(No, I'm Scottish.)*
d Chciałbym spotkać się z tobą. *(At what time?)*

Exercise 4

Complete the following sentences. Choose the correct answers from the selection in the box. (green cards)

a Chciałbym mieszkać _____.
b Nie muszę zobaczyć _____.
c Chciałabym zasięgnąć _____.
d Chciałbym mieć _____.
e Chciałbym zamówić _____.
f Chciałabym kupić _____.

> Kraków, przewodnik,   informacji,   psa,   w Krakowie,   kot,
> stolik,   informacja,   Wawelu,   Wawel

Did you know?

During World War II, Polish mathematician and cryptologist Marian Rejewski (1905–80) solved the general concept of how the famous German encrypting Enigma machine worked, thus giving the British cryptologists at Bletchley Park a head start in cracking the Enigma code and hugely contributing to the victory by Britain and Allied forces over Nazi Germany.

6

Poproszę lody
Can I have an ice cream, please?

In this unit you will learn
- *how to ask for things politely*
- *how to order food*
- *how to buy stamps and postcards*

In this unit you will learn how to ask for things politely – this is particularly useful when shopping or eating out.

Insight

Whenever possible, listen to the dialogues a few times without looking at the text. Then listen and follow the text in the book. Finally, try to read out loud along with the recording.

Dialogue 1 **Dialog pierwszy**

The following day Maria and Andrew are meeting for a coffee in one of many cafés in the beautiful Market Square in the heart of Kraków's Old Town. It's a busy place; the sound of horse-drawn carriages carrying tourists echoes across the square; the folk band plays traditional Polish music and the trumpeter is playing the traditional bugle-call (**hejnał**) from the tower of the **Kościół Mariacki** (St Mary's Church). A young waitress comes up to their table.

Vocabulary Słówka

Form in the dialogue	Dictionary form	English translation
sernik		*cheesecake*
lody kawowe	lód, lody, kawowy	*coffee ice cream*
a		*and* (with a change of participant), *and/but*
słucham państwa		*Can I help you?* (literally: *I'm listening to you, ladies and gentlemen*)

Kelnerka (waitress)	Dzień dobry. Słucham państwa?	*Hello. Can I help you?*
Maria	Poproszę kawę i sernik.	*Can I have a coffee and a cheesecake, please?*
Andrew	A ja poproszę herbatę i lody kawowe.	*And can I have a tea, and a coffee ice cream, please?*
Kelnerka	Proszę bardzo.	*Certainly.*

Dialogue 2 **Dialog drugi**

Maria and Andrew have finished their meal and Maria asks for the bill.

Vocabulary **Słówka**

Form in the dialogue	Dictionary form	English translation
rachunek		*bill*
zapłacić	płacić > zapłacić	*pay*
wykluczone	wykluczony; wykluczać > wykluczyć	*excluded, out of the question*
gościem	gość	*guest*

Maria	Poproszę rachunek.	*Can I have the bill, please?*
Kelnerka	Proszę.	*Here you are.*
Andrew	Chciałbym zapłacić rachunek.	*I would like to pay the bill.*
Maria	Wykluczone.	*Out of the question.*
	Jesteś moim gościem.	*You are my guest.*
Andrew	Dziękuję bardzo.	*Thank you very much.*

Dialogue 3 **Dialog trzeci**

Maria has paid the bill and she and Andrew leave the café. Andrew sees a small stall selling newspapers and postcards. He would like to send a postcard from Kraków to his family in England. He approaches the stall and chooses a postcard.

Vocabulary Słówka

Form in the dialogue	Dictionary form	English translation
tę	ta	*this*
widokówka		*postcard*
Ile płacę?	ile, płacić > zapłacić	*How much am I paying?/How much do I owe you?*
dwa pięćdziesiąt		*two fifty*

Andrew	Poproszę tę widokówkę.	*Can I have this postcard, please?*
Kobieta (woman)	Proszę.	*Certainly.*
Andrew	Ile płacę?	*How much do I owe you?*
Kobieta	Dwa pięćdziesiąt.	*Two fifty (two złoty fifty groszy).*

Dialogue 4 Dialog czwarty

Next, Andrew goes to the post office to buy a stamp.

Vocabulary Słówka

Form in the dialogue	Dictionary form	English translation
słucham	słuchać	*I'm listening/can I help?*
znaczek		*stamp*
zwykły		*ordinary, usual*
lotniczy		*airmail*
poproszę	prosić > poprosić	*I'll ask for/Can I have …?*
do + genitive		*to*
do Wielkiej Brytanii	Wielka Brytania	*to Great Britain*

Sprzedawca (male sales assistant)	Słucham?	*Can I help?*
Andrew	Poproszę znaczek do Wielkiej Brytanii.	*Can I have a stamp to Great Britain, please?*
Sprzedawca	Zwykły czy lotniczy?	*Normal or air mail?*
Andrew	Poproszę lotniczy.	*Air mail, please.*

Andrew asked for **znaczek lotniczy** (as opposed to **zwykły**). However, these days it is more common to ask for **znaczek priorytetowy** or **znaczek ekonomiczny**.

Let's practise

▶ Copy the dialogues (both Polish and English parts) onto small pieces of paper.
▶ Mix the pieces and reconstruct the dialogues correctly (both parts).
▶ Mix the pieces again and reconstruct the Polish side of the dialogues.
▶ Separate the Polish and English parts of the dialogues. Turn the Polish parts face down and mix them again. Turn them face up at random and translate into English.
▶ Do the same exercise with the English part of the dialogues.

How the language works

As you can see from the dialogues, **Poproszę** *Can I have ... please* is the key word if you would like to ask for something politely. Literally, it means *I'll ask for*; in practice it means *Can I have ... please?* Look at the following diagram and see how it works with a selection of masculine, feminine and neuter nouns as well as some nouns in the plural form.

Listen and repeat

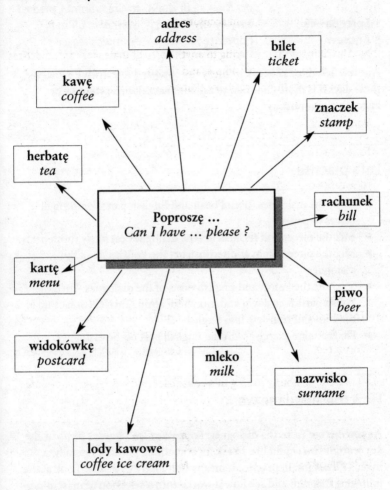

Using *Poproszę* gives you another opportunity to practise accusative forms.

We mentioned the accusative in Unit 3 when we talked about 'affirmative accusative' (vs. negative genitive when used in negative sentences).

Sentences like **Poproszę piwo** *Can I have a beer, please* are an excellent opportunity to practice using the accusative because **Poproszę** is followed by the direct object (*Can I have ... **what?***).

As a quick reminder, we form accusatives as follows:

▶ Masculine nouns referring to anything inanimate, and the adjectives with them, and neuter nouns, and the adjectives with them, don't change from their dictionary citation (nominative) forms.

Nominative	Accusative
To jest rachunek.	Poproszę rachunek.
This is the bill.	*Can I have the bill, please?*
To jest piwo.	Poproszę piwo.
This is beer.	*Can I have beer, please?*

▶ Feminine nouns ending in -a change the -a to -ę.

Nominative	Accusative
To jest kanapka.	Poproszę kanapkę.
This is a sandwich.	*Can I have a sandwich, please?*
To jest herbata.	Poproszę herbatę.
This is tea.	*Can I have (some) tea, please?*

▶ Masculine nouns ending in a consonant and referring to animate beings typically add -a.

Nominative	Accusative
To jest jeden syn.	Mam jednego syna.
This is one son.	*I have one son.*
To jest czarny kot.	Mam czarnego kota.
This is a black cat.	*I have a black cat.*

Pronunciation guide **Jak to wymówić?**

What gives Polish its distinctive sound and its fearsome reputation is the frequency of combinations of three and sometimes even four consonants without a vowel between them. On paper the fearsome reputation is enhanced by the fact that some consonant sounds are represented by pairs of consonant letters. Anyone who thinks that **y** is also a consonant letter is going to think some Polish words consist entirely of consonants; **czyść** actually consists of consonant **cz**, vowel **y**, and finally consonants **ś** and **ć**.

Here are some examples of common consonant combinations, with spellings given between < > and pronunciation guidance given using Polish spelling between [ ]:

<prz> or <psz>	[p-sz]*	as in **przepraszam** *(excuse me)*, **przykry** *(unpleasant)*, **wieprz** *(hog)*, **pszenica** *(wheat)*
<krz> or <ksz>	[k-sz]	as in **krzyczeć** (shout), **krzew** (shrub), **większy** *(bigger)*
<trz> or <tsz>	[t-sz] or [cz–sz]	as in **trzeba** *(you need to)*, **trzy** *(three)*, **trzoda** *(livestock)*, **trzcina** [t–sz-cina] *(reeds)*, **gorętszy** *(hotter)*
<szcz> or <żdż>	[sz-cz]	as in **Leszczyński** *(Polish surname)*, **deszcz** *(rain)*, or **drożdże** *(yeast)*
<żdż>	[ż-dż]	as in **drożdżówka** *(teacake/bun)*, **przyjeżdżać** *(arrive)*
<chrz> or <ch–sz>	[ch-sz]	as in **chrzan** *(horsradish)*, **chrząszcz** *(beetle)*, **chrześcijański** *(Christian)*
<skrz>	[s-k-sz]	as in **skrzypce** *(violin)*

*Note: You may be puzzled why the **prz** combination is pronunced [psz] and not [pż] – it's all to do with the process which is called de-voicing and will be explained in the next unit.

There are two more common combinations:

▶ [s-ch] as in **schody** (*stairs*), **wyschnąć** (*to dry*)
▶ [t-ch] as in **tchórz** (*coward*), **natchnienie** (*inspiration*).

Here are a couple of examples involving soft consonants:

| <ść> or <źdź> | [ś-ć] | as in **kość** (*bone*), **dość** (*enough*), **gwóźdź** (*nail*) |
| <źdź> | [ź-dź] | as in **źdźbło** (*blade of grass*), **jeździć** (*to go*) |

Don't be frightened by these letter combinations. English, in fact, has similar examples: when we say *Can I cash cheques here?* and *Is there any fresh cheese?* we produce combinations much like Polish [szcz] and [śĉ], and when we say *It's time to shut up shop* we produce a combination like the [psz] at the beginning of **Przepraszam**.

Test yourself

Exercise 1

Translate the following sentences into Polish. (blue cards)

a Can I have a coffee, please?
b Can I have (a piece of) cheesecake, please?
c I'd like to pay the bill, please.
d Out of the question.
e You are my guest.
f Can I have a postcard, please?
g Can I have an airmail stamp to Great Britain, please?
h How much (am I paying)?

Exercise 2

Translate the following sentences into Polish. (blue cards)

a Can I have a tea, please?
b I'd like some tea, please.
c Can I have a coffee, please?
d I'd like some coffee, please.
e Can I have a stamp, please?
f I'd like to buy a stamp.
g Can I have a guidebook, please?
h I'd like to buy a guidebook.
i Can I have the bill, please?
j I'd like to pay the bill.

Exercise 3

What's wrong with the sentences below? (green cards)

a Barbara jest emerytem.
b Andrew jest Polką.
c Poproszę kawa.
d Chciałbym zamówić znaczek.
e Jestem dwadzieścia lat.
f Mam ochotę na herbata.
g Musi pan koniecznie kupić Wawel.

◄⑴ CD1, TR 46

Exercise 4

Respond in Polish to the following questions and statements using the English prompts. You can check your answers and practise pronunciation on the recording. (yellow cards)

a Poproszę rachunek.
(Here you are.)

b Słucham panią/paną?
(Can I have a coffee, please?)

c Chciał(a)bym zapłacić rachunek.
(Out of the question. You are my guest.)

d Ile płacę?
(Two złoty and fifty groszy.)

Did you know? (purple cards)

▶ In the seventeenth century, the Polish Commonwealth was the largest state in Europe. It covered 990,000 km^2; it stretched from the Baltic Sea to the Black Sea and covered the area which today belongs to Poland, Lithuania, Latvia, Estonia, Russia, Belarus, Ukraine, Slovakia, the Czech Republic, Hungary, Moldova and Romania. The country shared a border with the Ottoman Empire (Turkey). Poland was the original 'East meets West'.

▶ Poland was the most religiously tolerant country in Europe. It was the first country where religious freedom was guaranteed by an Act of Parliament (Warsaw Confederation 1573).

▶ The fashion for Persian carpets in wealthy European houses was introduced by Poles.

7

Lubię kuchnię polską
I like Polish cuisine

In this unit you will learn
- *how to express likes and dislikes*
- *how to say what you like and/or don't like doing*
- *how to talk about your favourite cuisine*

In this unit you'll learn how to express likes and dislikes.

Dialogue 1 **Dialog pierwszy**

Andrew and Maria have spent the morning in the Archives. They're both hungry and Maria suggests going for lunch.

Vocabulary **Słówka**

Form in the dialogue	Dictionary form	English translation
głodny		*hungry*
trochę		*a bit*
chodźmy	chodzić > pochodzić	*let's go*
obiad		*lunch, dinner*
kuchnia		*kitchen, cooking, cuisine, food*

bigos	*bigos – traditional Polish cabbage stew known as 'hunter's stew'*
piwo	*beer/lager*

Andrew	Jestem trochę głodny.	*I'm a bit hungry.*
Maria	Chodźmy na obiad.	*Let's go for lunch.*
	Czy lubi pan kuchnię polską?	*Do you like Polish cooking?*
Andrew	Tak, lubię bigos, sernik i polskie piwo.	*Yes, I like bigos, cheesecake and Polish beer.*

CD1, TR 47

Dialogue 2 **Dialog drugi**

Maria and Andrew walk along Grodzka Street towards the Wawel Hill. A five-minute walk away they find the *Pod Aniołami* restaurant. They go in. While waiting for the order to arrive, they carry on talking. Maria asks Andrew what he'd like to see in Kraków.

Vocabulary **Słówka**

Form in the dialogue	Dictionary form	English translation
zobaczyć	widzieć > zobaczyć	*see*
rynek		*market*
Sukiennice (plural)		*the Cloth Hall*
narodowe	narodowy	*national*

Maria	Co chciałby pan zobaczyć w Krakowie?	*What would you like to see in Kraków?*
Andrew	Chciałbym zobaczyć Rynek, Sukiennice, Wawel i Muzeum Narodowe.	*I'd like to see the Market Square, the Cloth Hall, the Wawel castle and the National Museum.*

CD1, TR 48

Dialogue 3 Dialog trzeci

Maria's keen to find out about Andrew's taste in art.

Vocabulary Słówka

Form in the dialogue	Dictionary form	English translation
obrazy	obraz	*paintings*
pytać o + acc.	pytać > zapytać	*ask about*
dlaczego		*why*
słynny		*famous*
łasiczką	łasiczka	*little weasel**
dama		*lady*
chętnie	chętny	*willingly, with pleasure*
zwiedzać	zwiedzać > zwiedzić	*visit (places, things)*
galerie	galeria	*galleries*
muzea	muzeum	*museums*

CD1, TR 49

Maria	Czy lubi pan obrazy Leonarda da Vinci?	*Do you like paintings by Leonardo da Vinci?*
Andrew	Tak, bardzo. Dlaczego pani pyta?	*Yes, very much so. Why are you asking?*
Maria	W Krakowie jest słynny obraz Leonarda Dama z łasiczką. Czy chciałby pan go zobaczyć?	*In Kraków there is a famous painting by Leonardo, Lady with a little weasel. Would you like to see it?*
Andrew	Bardzo chętnie. Lubię zwiedzać galerie i muzea.	*I'd love to. I like visiting galleries and museums.*

*The famous painting by Leonardo is commonly and incorrectly referred to as 'Dama z łasiczką' (*Lady with a little weasel*) while official guidebooks and other publications refer to it by its proper title: 'Dama z gronostajem' (*Lady with an Ermine*). Whatever the name, the painting is well worth seeing.

82

Let's practise

▶ Copy the dialogues (both Polish and English parts) onto small pieces of paper.
▶ Mix the pieces and reconstruct the dialogues correctly (both parts).
▶ Mix the pieces again and reconstruct the Polish side of the dialogues.
▶ Separate Polish and English parts of the dialogues. Turn the Polish parts face down and mix them again. Turn them face up at random and translate into English.
▶ Do the same exercise with the English part of the dialogues.
▶ Arrange the Polish side of the dialogue in the correct order, turn Andrew's part face down and try to speak his part without looking.
▶ Repeat the same exercises with Maria's part.

Insight

Successful language learning is about practice, repetition and revision. It's important that from time to time you go back to the beginning of the course to read and listen to all the dialogues in one go. It will give you a better experience of listening to and reading in Polish and it will help you to tune into the melody and rhythm of the language.

Kuchnia polska/indyjska/chińska/francuska i włoska

Andrew likes Polish cuisine. He mentions **bigos** (*hunter's stew*), a Polish speciality, **sernik** (*cheesecake*) and Polish beer. In Polish the same word **piwo** describes both *beer* and *lager*. Possibly the most famous Polish brand is Żywiec, frequently seen now among the many Polish beers on sale in English pubs. If you like beer you can say **Lubię piwo**. If you like a particular brand of beer you can say: **Lubię Żywiec/Okocim/Tyskie/Lecha**.

After the collapse of communism, Poland became a magnet for chefs and restaurateurs from all over the world. In big cities you can find a vast range of restaurants offering different types of cuisine: Chinese, Indian, Italian, French, etc.

Let's practise saying what your taste in cuisine is:

Types of cuisine		I like ... cuisine	
kuchnia	polska	*Polish*	Lubię kuchnię polską.
	indyjska	*Indian*	Lubię kuchnię indyjską.
	chińska	*Chinese*	Lubię kuchnię chińską.
	włoska	*Italian*	Lubię kuchnię włoską.
	francuska	*French*	Lubię kuchnię francuską.
	meksykańska	*Mexican*	Lubię kuchnię meksykańską.
	hiszpańska	*Spanish*	Lubię kuchnię hiszpańską.
	tajwańska	*Taiwanese*	Lubię kuchnię tajwańską.
	tajlandza	*Thai*	Lubię kuchnię tajlandzką.
	grecka	*Greek*	Lubię kuchnię grecką.

Preferably with a friend, practise saying what types of cuisine you like in a short dialogue:

X   Czy lubisz kuchnię polską (indyjską, etc.)?

Y   Tak, lubię.

or

Y   Nie, nie lubię.

How the language works

◀) CD1, TR 51

Adjectives and nouns

The expression **kuchnia polska** illustrates an important principle in Polish related to the order in which adjectives and nouns can appear. In Polish, just like English, nouns can follow adjectives:

zły pies	*vicious dog*
ciekawa książka	*an interesting book*
piękny obraz	*a beautiful picture/painting*
nowy samochód	*a new car*

But if the noun refers to a different thing when accompanied by a different adjective (forming a different vocabulary item, if you like), the order will be reversed and the noun will precede its adjective. This doesn't refer to cuisine that happens to be Polish, or that some people might regard as Polish; it refers to Polish cuisine as opposed to any other kind of cuisine (French, Indian, Chinese, etc.).

In other words, the adjective placed after the noun will distinguish between different types of cuisine. Here are some more examples which illustrate the point.

Listen and repeat

lekcja	pierwsza	*Lesson 1*
dialog	drugi	*Dialogue 2*
gabinet	okulistyczny	*optician's*
gabinet	dentystyczny	*dentist's*
gabinet	kosmetyczny	*beauty salon*
kawiarnia	internetowa	*internet café*
akademia	medyczna	*medical school*
akademia	rolnicza	*agricultural college*
aparat	słuchowy	*hearing aid*
aparat	fotograficzny	*camera*

język	polski	*Polish language*
język	angielski	*English language*
język	obcy	*foreign language*
firma	handlowa	*trading company*
firma	budowlana	*building firm*
salon	fryzjerski	*hairdresser's*
salon	samochodowy	*car showroom*
straż	miejska	*town guard*
straż	pożarna	*fire brigade*
straż	więzienna	*prison officers*
szkoła	podstawowa	*primary school*
szkoła	średnia	*secondary school*
usługi	kserograficzne	*photocopying*
usługi	szewskie	*shoe repair*
usługi	pogrzebowe	*funeral services, undertaker's*
dworzec	kolejowy	*railway station*
dworzec	autobusowy	*bus/coach station*

For example, **nowy gabinet** (adjective + noun) is a **gabinet** (*surgery*, *salon*, *study*) that happens at the moment to be new, whereas a **gabinet dentystyczny** (noun + adjective) is a *dental surgery*, a **gabinet okulistyczny** (also noun + adjective) is an *optician's* and a **gabinet kosmetyczny** is a *beauty salon*, new or not.

Co lubisz? Co lubisz robić? *What do you like? What do you like doing?*

In English you can use *like* with a noun as its direct object (*I like coffee*) or with an *-ing* form of a verb (*I like drinking coffee*), or with an infinitive (*I like to leave the tastiest thing till last*). Similarly, in Polish you can say **Lubię kawę** and **Lubię pić kawę**. The form **pić** is an infinitive, the basic dictionary form of the verb. Here are some more examples:

Lubię obrazy Leonarda.	*I like paintings by Leonardo.*
Lubię oglądać obrazy Leonarda.	*I like looking at paintings by Leonardo.*
Lubię galerie i muzea.	*I like galleries and museums.*
Lubię zwiedzać galerie i muzea.	*I like visiting galleries and museums.*

Here's what **lubić** looks like for all persons in singular and plural:

ja	lubię	Lubię galerie.	*I like galleries.*
		Lubię zwiedzać galerie.	*I like visiting galleries.*
ty	lubisz	Lubisz galerie	*You like galleries.*
		Lubisz zwiedzać galerie.	*You like visiting galleries.*
on	lubi		
ona	lubi	On/ona/ono lubi galerie.	*S/he/it likes galleries.*
ono	lubi	On/ona/ono lubi zwiedzać galerie.	*S/he/it likes visiting galleries.*
pan/pani	lubi	Pan/pani lubi galerie.	*Sir/madam likes galleries.*
		Pan/pani lubi zwiedzać galerie.	*Sir/madam likes visiting galleries.*
my	lubimy	Lubimy galerie.	*We like galleries.*
		Lubimy zwiedzać galerie.	*We like visiting galleries.*
wy	lubicie	Lubicie galerie.	*You like galleries.*
		Lubicie zwiedzać galerie.	*You like visiting galleries.*
oni	lubią	Oni/one lubią galerie.	*They like galleries.*
one	lubią	Oni/one lubią zwiedzać galerie.	*They like visiting galleries.*
panowie/ panie/ państwo	lubią	Panowie/panie lubią galerie.	*Gentlemen/ladies like galleries.*
		Państwo lubią galerie.	*Ladies and gentlemen like galleries.*
		Panowie/panie lubią zwiedzać galerie.	*Gentlemen/ladies like visiting galleries.*
		Państwo lubią zwiedzać galerie.	*Ladies and gentlemen like visiting galleries.*

Listen and repeat

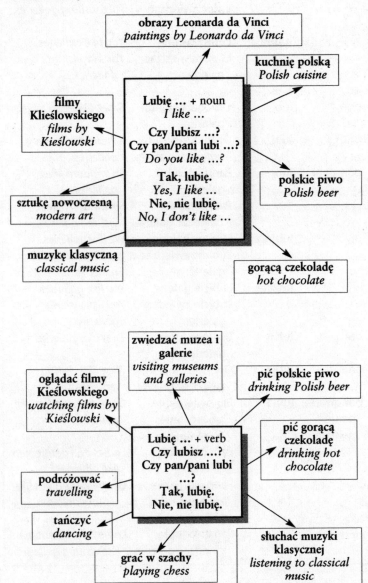

obrazy Leonarda da Vinci
paintings by Leonardo da Vinci

kuchnię polską
Polish cuisine

filmy Klieślowskiego
films by Kieślowski

Lubię … + noun
I like …

Czy lubisz …?
Czy pan/pani lubi …?
Do you like …?

Tak, lubię.
Yes, I like …
Nie, nie lubię.
No, I don't like …

polskie piwo
Polish beer

sztukę nowoczesną
modern art

muzykę klasyczną
classical music

gorącą czekoladę
hot chocolate

zwiedzać muzea i galerie
visiting museums and galleries

oglądać filmy Kieślowskiego
watching films by Kieślowski

pić polskie piwo
drinking Polish beer

Lubię … + verb
Czy lubisz …?
Czy pan/pani lubi …?
Tak, lubię.
Nie, nie lubię.

pić gorącą czekoladę
drinking hot chocolate

podróżować
travelling

tańczyć
dancing

grać w szachy
playing chess

słuchać muzyki klasycznej
listening to classical music

Pronunciation guide **Jak to wymówić?**

Voiced and voiceless consonants

From previous units you know that Polish consonants can be divided into two groups: soft consonants and hard consonants. But for a select group of consonants (listed in the table below) there is another division. These consonants can also be divided into two groups according to how they are produced: *voiced* or *voiceless*. Every voiced consonant has its voiceless counterpart. So which ones are which?

Voiced consonants	Voiceless consonants
b	p
d	t
g	k
w	f
z	s
ż	sz
rz*	sz
dż	cz
dź	ć

*A quick reminder that two letter combinations (**ch, rz, sz, cz, dz, dż** and **dź**) represent one sound and equal one consonant.

What's the difference between voiced and voiceless consonants?

Voiced consonants are those that vibrate the vocal chords as the sound is pronounced. Their corresponding voiceless consonants use the same shape of the mouth to pronounce the sound but without causing the vocal chords to vibrate.

If you place two fingers (index and middle finger) on the voice box (i.e. the location of the Adam's apple in the upper throat) you can feel a vibration when you pronounce *zzzzzzzzz* (voiced) but not when you pronounce *sssss* (voiceless).

If you imagine voiced and voiceless consonants as partners, it's the voiceless ones which are more powerful and influential because they can alter how voiced consonants behave and turn them into voiceless ones. This process is called de-voicing and it's very common in Polish. It can happen at the end of a word or in the middle of a word. Let me give you some examples:

If a word ends in a voiced consonant (**b, d, z, w, g**, etc.) it will be pronounced with the voiceless counterpart. For example, **ogród** (*garden*) – although **d** is voiced it is pronounced [ogrut] with **t**, **d**'s voiceless counterpart.

Listen and repeat

le<u>w</u>	*lion*	[le<u>f</u>]
chle<u>b</u>	*bread*	[chle<u>p</u>] (remember **ch** = *h* as in *loch*)
grzy<u>b</u>	*mushroom*	[g<u>ż</u>y<u>p</u>]
obia<u>d</u>	*dinner*	[obia<u>t</u>]
d<u>ąb</u>	*oak*	[dom<u>p</u>]
pa<u>w</u>	*peacock*	[pa<u>f</u>]
twar<u>z</u>	*face*	[tfa<u>sz</u>]

The last example also demonstrates de-voicing in the middle of the word (as well as at the end).

W and **rz** are always pronounced as [f] and [sz] when they follow a voiceless consonant:

▶ **Prz** [psz]: **przepraszam** (*excuse me*), **przykry** (*unpleasant*), **przyloty** (*arrivals*)

▶ **Trz** [tsz]: **trzeba** (*you need to*), **trzaskać** (*slam*), **trząść** (*shake*),

▶ **Chrz** [chsz]: **chrząszcz** (*beetle*), **chrzan** (*horseradish*), **chrząkać** (*to hum*)

▶ **Krz** [ksz]: **krzesło** (*chair*), **krzak** (*shrub*), **krzyczeć** (*shout*)

▶ **Wrz** [wsz]: **wszystko** (*everything*), **wszelki** (*every*), **wszy** (*flees*)

▶ **Tw** [tf]: **twarz** (*face*), **twój** (*your*), **twardy** (*hard*)

▶ **Kw** [kf]: **kwadrat** (*square*), **kwartał** (*quarter of the year*), **kwarc** (*quartz*)

▶ **Sw** [sf]: **swój** (*one's own*), **swoboda** (*freedom*), **Swarzędz** [sfażenc] (*Polish town*).

De-voicing is so common in Polish that Poles speaking English find it almost impossible not to do it. To an average Polish ear there's no difference between *food* and *foot*, both will be pronounce as [fut]. Needless to say, it may lead to some interesting conversations with Poles who encourage you to eat some delicious *foot*.

Test yourself

Exercise 1

Translate the following sentences into Polish. (blue cards)

a I'm a bit hungry.
b Do you like Polish cuisine?
c Yes, I like Polish beer/lager.
d What would you like to see in Kraków?
e I'd like to see the Market square and the Cloth Hall.
f Do you like visiting galleries and museums?
g I like paintings by Leonardo da Vinci.
h There is a famous painting by Leonardo in Kraków.
i Would you like to see the painting?
j I like Chinese cuisine but I don't like Indian cuisine.

Exercise 2

Complete the following sentences. (green cards)

a Lubię _____ polskie piwo.
b Czy lubi pani pić gorącą _____ ?
c Maria lubi _____ muzyki klasycznej.
d Andrew lubi _____ tango.

e Czy lubisz _____ muzea?

f Lubię _____ filmy Kieślowskiego.

g Tomek lubi _____ w szachy.

Exercise 3

Match the verbs on the left with the appropriate nouns on the right.

1	słuchać	**a**	informacji
2	tańczyć	**b**	galerię
3	jeść	**c**	tango
4	pić	**d**	widokówkę
5	oglądać	**e**	muzyki
6	zwiedzać	**f**	stolik
7	zobaczyć	**g**	po polsku
8	mieć	**h**	owoce
9	mieszkać	**i**	psa
10	mówić	**j**	herbatę
11	zamówić	**k**	w Krakowie
12	zasięgnąć	**l**	film
13	kupić	**m**	Rynek

◄) CD2, TR 2

Exercise 4

Respond to the following in Polish. Check if your answers and pronunciation are correct on the recording. (yellow cards)

a Czy lubisz obrazy Leonarda?
(Yes, I do (like).)

b Czy lubisz zwiedzać muzea i galerie?
(No, I don't (like).)

c Co chciałbyś zobaczyć w Krakowie?
(I'd like to see the Mariacki church.)

d Jaką kuchnię lubisz?
(I like Polish and Italian cuisine.)

Did you know? (purple cards)

Polish hospitality is legendary. 'A guest in the home: God in the home' is the saying that many Poles hold dear. Poles will go to extraordinary lengths, including debt, to show themselves as good hosts. During the deep economic crisis of the 1980s, when most food stuffs were only available on rations and long queues were the most memorable image of Poland, foreigners were often stunned by how much food was put on the table by their Polish hosts. Most foreign guests were completely oblivious to the fact that the whole family and even the entire neighbourhood would have had to collect their rations for weeks to provide this level of hospitality.

Insight

So far you have learned how to introduce yourself and others; how to describe your family, other people, objects and animals; how to say you must do something; express what you have and haven't got; what your likes and dislikes are. It's quite a lot. Try to put it all together and prepare a short story about yourself. Use photos, pictures or internet web sites – anything that will help you to tell others who you are. Don't be too ambitious though – remember to use the language you've learned. Try to start thinking in Polish rather then constantly translating from English to Polish. Be positive and think how much you can say rather than how much you don't know yet and remember there is plenty of time to learn new things in the remaining eight units.

8

Można, trzeba, wolno, warto
One can, one needs to, it's allowed, it's worth

In this unit you will learn
- *how to ask for permission*
- *how to say what needs to be done*
- *how to say what is and is not allowed*
- *how to say what is worth doing*

In this unit you will learn how to ask for permission, express and understand what needs to be done, what is and is not allowed, and what is worth doing.

Dialogue 1 Dialog pierwszy

Maria takes Andrew to the Muzeum Czartoryskich to see the famous painting *Dama z tasiczką* by Leonardo da Vinci. Andrew sees many interesting objects he would like to take photographs of. He enquires if he is allowed to take photos in the museum.

Vocabulary Słówka

Form in the dialogue	Dictionary form	English translation
wolno		*it's allowed, one may*
robić zdjęcia	robić > zrobić; zdjęcie	*take photographs*
przykro mi	przykry, ja	*I'm sorry*
szkoda		*pity, shame*

Andrew	Czy wolno robić zdjęcia w muzeum?	*Is taking photos allowed in the museum?*
Maria	Nie, nie wolno. Przykro mi.	*No, it's not allowed. I'm sorry.*
Andrew	Szkoda.	*Pity.*

Dialogue 2 **Dialog drugi**

Buying a guidebook is perhaps his next best option.

Vocabulary **Słówka**

Form in the dialogue	Dictionary form	English translation
gdzie		*where*
przewodnik		*guidebook*
w + locative		*in*
w sklepie muzealnym	sklep, muzealny	*in the museum shop*
jeszcze		*still, besides, another*
można		*it's possible to*
książki	książka	*books*
albumy	album	*albums*
plakaty	plakat	*posters*
zakładki	zakładka	*bookmarks*
magnesy	magnes	*(fridge) magnets*
pocztówki	pocztówka	*postcard*
itd. (i tak dalej)		*etc.*
kupić	kupować > kupić	*buy*
znaczki	znaczek	*stamps*
nie wiem	wiedzieć	*I don't know*
trzeba		*one needs to/ you need to*
zapytać	pytać > zapytać	*ask*

Andrew	Gdzie można kupić przewodnik?	*Where can you buy a guidebook?*
Maria	W sklepie muzealnym.	*In the museum shop.*
Andrew	Co jeszcze można tam kupić?	*What else can you buy there?*
Maria	Książki, albumy, plakaty, zakładki, magnesy, pocztówki itd.	*Books, coffee table books, posters, bookmarks, magnets, postcards, etc.*

Andrew	A czy można kupić znaczki?	*And can you buy stamps?*
Maria	Nie wiem.	*I don't know.*
	Trzeba zapytać.	*You need to ask.*

Dialogue 3 **Dialog trzeci**

Andrew asks how to get to the gift shop.

Vocabulary **Słówka**

Form in the dialogue	Dictionary form	English translation
wyjść	wychodzić > wyjść	*go out, come out*
z muzeum		*from/out of the museum*
przejść	przechodzić > przejść	*go/come through, go/come across*
korytarzem	korytarz	*along the corridor*
do sklepu	sklep	*to the shop*
prosto	prosty	*straight*
po + locative		*after, along, by*
po schodach	schody	*by the stairs, along the stairs*
w dół		*downwards*
na + locative		*(located) on, at*
na parterze	parter	*on the ground floor (American first floor)*
warto		*worth*

◆ CD2, TR 5

Andrew	Gdzie jest sklep?	*Where is the shop?*
	Czy trzeba wyjść z muzeum?	*Do you need to leave the museum?*
Maria	Nie, można przejść korytarzem do sklepu.	*No, you can go along the corridor to the shop.*
	Trzeba iść prosto, potem	*You need to go straight ahead,*

	po schodach w dół.	*then down the stairs.*
	Sklep jest na parterze.	*The shop is on the ground floor.*
Andrew	Co jeszcze warto kupić w sklepie?	*What else is worth buying in the shop?*

Dialogue 4 **Dialog czwarty**

Andrew has bought a coffee table book, a guidebook and a few bookmarks. He would like to pay for them.

Vocabulary **Słówka**

Form in the dialogue	**Dictionary form**	**English translation**
kartą kredytową	karta kredytowa	*by credit card*
zapłacić za + acc.	płacić > zapłacić	*pay for*

Andrew	Przepraszam, czy można zapłacić kartą kredytową?	*Excuse me, can you pay by credit card?*
Sales assistant	Tak, można.	*Yes, you can.*

Let's practise

▶ Copy the dialogues (both the Polish and English parts) onto small pieces of paper.

▶ Mix the pieces and reconstruct the dialogues correctly (both parts).

▶ Mix the pieces again and reconstruct the Polish side of the dialogues.

▶ Separate the Polish and English parts of the dialogues. Turn the Polish parts face down and mix them again. Turn them face up at random and translate into English.

▶ Do the same exercise with the English parts of the dialogues.

Money, money, money

Andrew uses his credit card (**kartą kredytową**) as an instrument to pay for what he has bought. This is a perfect illustration of the instrumental case. You will find more about the instrumental case in the Grammar appendix.

◀)) CD2, TR 7

If credit cards are not accepted, what's the alternative?

gotówka	*cash* (Note: The Polish currency is złoty and grosz; 1 złoty = 100 groszy)
Czy można zapłacić gotówką?	*Can you pay in cash?*
czek	*cheque*
Czy można zapłacić czekiem?	*Can you pay by cheque?*
czek podróżny	*traveller's cheque*
Czy można zapłacić czekiem (podróżnym)?	*Can you pay by traveller's cheque?*
reszta	*change*
bankomat	*cash machine*

How the language works

Można, trzeba, wolno, warto *One can, one needs to, it's allowed, it's worth*

These are words you will hear a lot in Polish. We've grouped them here not just because you can use them in similar situations, as in the dialogues, but also because they are relatively easy to apply in everyday conversations. Poles often use them because they are a neat way of avoiding addressing the person you are speaking to; a bit like using *one* in English as in *Is one allowed to take photographs?* The difference is that in Polish it doesn't sound anywhere near as pompous as in English. In fact, it is frequently used in everyday Polish.

Można, trzeba, wolno and **warto** are always followed by a verb in its basic (infinitive) form:

Można robić zdjęcia.	*One can take photographs.*
Trzeba pojechać autobusem.	*You need to go by bus.*
Wolno wejść.	*You can go/come in.*
Warto zobaczyć katedrę.	*It's worth seeing the cathedral.*

Plurals

When Maria explains to Andrew what is in the museum shop to buy, she lists a number of things:

książki	*books*
albumy	*coffee table books*
zakładki	*bookmarks*

All these nouns are in the plural form, i.e. there are more than one of them. Polish has rather complicated rules which govern how plural forms are created. However, this shouldn't stop us from getting to know at least some of them.

To start with, it matters if a noun is masculine, feminine or neuter. Just to refresh your memory – feminine nouns usually end in -a, neuter nouns usually end in -e or -o and masculine nouns usually end in a consonant (**l**, **t**, **k**, etc.). Let's look at a selection of masculine nouns, which have appeared in the course so far:

Listen and repeat

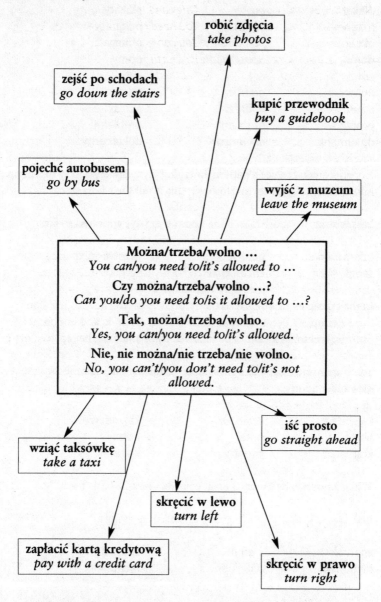

robić zdjęcia
take photos

zejść po schodach
go down the stairs

kupić przewodnik
buy a guidebook

pojechać autobusem
go by bus

wyjść z muzeum
leave the museum

Można/trzeba/wolno …
You can/you need to/it's allowed to …

Czy można/trzeba/wolno …?
Can you/do you need to/is it allowed to …?

Tak, można/trzeba/wolno.
Yes, you can/you need to/it's allowed.

Nie, nie można/nie trzeba/nie wolno.
No, you can't/you don't need to/it's not allowed.

iść prosto
go straight ahead

wziąć taksówkę
take a taxi

skręcić w lewo
turn left

zapłacić kartą kredytową
pay with a credit card

skręcić w prawo
turn right

Masculine singular form	English	Plural form
album	*coffee table book*	albumy
plakat	*poster*	plakaty
magnes	*magnet*	magnesy
obraz	*painting*	obrazy
dom	*house/home*	domy
kot	*cat*	koty
numer	*number*	numery
adres	*address*	adresy
problem	*problem*	problemy
dokument	*document*	dokumenty

Hopefully, you can see a pattern emerging – you simply add -y to a noun in the basic, singular form. However, this is not the whole story.

Let's look at two more masculine nouns that have appeared so far:

przewodnik	*guide(book)*	przewodniki
sernik	*cheesecake*	serniki

In the examples an -i replaced the -y. So why do you have to use -i in these examples? Because the singular form ends in -k, and in Polish, for historical reasons -k cannot be followed by -y and must be replaced by -i.

There are some more rules governing the formation of plurals of masculine nouns:

kalendarz	*calendar*	kalendarze
hotel	*hotel*	hotele
kraj	*country*	kraje

When a noun ends in -rz, -l or -j, you add -e to the basic form.

Let's have a look at a fourth group of masculine nouns:

znaczek	*stamp*	znaczki
rachunek	*bill*	rachunki

At first glance there is nothing remarkable about these examples, they seem to belong to the same category as **przewodniki** and **serniki** but there's a difference: they lose the -**e** from the ending -**ek** in **znaczek** and **rachunek**.

But before you feel completely overwhelmed by the number of different rules governing plurals, remember that the best way to learn is by collecting examples, forming word associations and learning in context. With experience you'll develop a form of intuition that will help you make an educated guess even if you don't know the answer for sure.

We will return to look at some more examples of plural nouns for feminine and neuter nouns in Unit 11.

◆) **CD2, TR 9**

Pronunciation guide Jak to wymówić?

Assimilation

Assimilation occurs when usually a voiceless consonant influences the consonant(s) before it.

Where two consonants occur in succession, the second one usually decides whether the combination is voiced or not, but **w** and **rz** are pronounced like **f** and **sz** when they follow a voiceless consonant:

wódka	[wutka]	*vodka*
książka	[ksiąszka]	*book*
w sieci	[fsieci]	*on/in the net*
w futrze	[ffutsze]	*in a fur*
w hotelu	[fhotelu]	*in a hotel*
swój	[sfuj]	*one's own*

In many Poles' Polish, this tendency even extends across the boundary between words, causing the last consonant of a word to become voiced, or preventing its de-voicing.

| To kot. | [to kOt] | *It's a cat.* |
| To kod. | [to kOt] | *It's a code.* |

but

kot był	[kodbył]	*The cat was ...*
kod był	[kodbył]	*The code was ...*
sześć miesięcy	[szeź(d)źmiesiency]	*six months*
tak zwany	[tagzwany]	*so called*

Listen for this when you listen to Poles talking. Listen for it on the recording and imitate it, as it all helps towards smoothness and fluency.

Try these examples:

stwórca	[stf]	*creator*
także	[gż]	*also*
wódka	[tk]	*vodka*
książka	[szk]	*book*

A confusing 'ck' combination

English native speakers find a common Polish combination of letters c and k a little confusing. This is probably because it is also a common letter combination in English where it is pronounced as a single sound [k] as in *pack*, *track*, *muck*. In Polish the pronunciation is different. You need to pronounce both c [ts] and k separately. The combination will often be followed by -i or -a. This combination commonly appears in Polish surnames:

Buczacki	Buczacka
Krasicki	Krasicka
Mędrzycki	Mędrzycka
Mościcki	Mościcka

This letter combination also appears in some adjectives such as:

niemiecki	*German*
szlachecki	*of Polish gentry*
karpacki	*Carpathian*

Test yourself

Exercise 1

Write down the plural forms of the following nouns. (green cards)

a	telefon	*telephone*
b	komputer	*computer*
c	samochód	*car*
d	stolik	*small table*
e	słownik	*dictionary*
f	ręcznik	*towel*
g	murarz	*brick layer*

Exercise 2

Translate the following sentences into Polish. (blue cards)

a Is taking photos allowed in the museum?
b I'm sorry but it's not allowed.
c Pity.
d Can you buy a guidebook in the museum shop?
e What else can you buy there?
f You can buy books and bookmarks there.
g Where is the shop?
h Do you need to leave the museum?
i The shop is on the ground floor.
j You need to go straight on.
k Excuse me, can you pay by credit card?
l I'm sorry but you can't.
m What else is worth buying?

Exercise 3

Respond to the following statements and questions in Polish. You can practice your pronunciation and check the answers on the recording. (yellow cards)

a Czy wolno robić zdjęcia w muzeum?
   (No, it's not allowed.)
b Gdzie jest sklep?
   (On the ground floor.)
c Gdzie można kupić przewodnik?
   (In the museum shop.)
d Czy można kupić znaczki w sklepie muzealnym?
   (I don't know; you need to ask.)
e Co chciałby pan zwiedzić w Krakowie?
   (I'd like to see Wawel.)
f Musimy spotkać się jutro (tomorrow).
   (I'd love to.)

Exercise 4

Complete the following sentences. (green cards)

a Chciałbym _____ zdjęcia w galerii.
b Gdzie jest _____ muzealny?
c Czy mogę zapłacić _____ _____?
d Sklep jest na _____.
e Co można _____ w sklepie muzealnym?
f Trzeba przejść _____ do sklepu.
g Trzeba zejść po _____ w dół.
h Czy trzeba skręcić w _____ czy w _____?

Did you know? (purple cards)
Dwory and *dworki*

One of the most striking things in Poland today is the number of new houses. You can easily get the impression that there are no old traditional houses at all. But this is not the case.

Polish country houses (**dworki**) and small stately homes (**dwory**) are one of the keys to understanding the spirit of Poland, Polish culture, heritage and history. Built in a traditional way and inhabited by **szlachta** (Polish gentry), **dwory** were the centre of family, social and patriotic life. They were full of books, armoury and weapons brought back from military campaigns, hunting trophies and portraits of ancestors. At the time of the Partitions, when Poland ceased to exist as an independent country and was partitioned by Russia, Prussia and the Austro-Hungarian Empire, **dwory** and **dworki** became the guardians of Polish survival.

Before World War II, there were approximately 13,000 such residences all over Poland. Under communism they were neglected, vandalized and slowly decayed. After the collapse of communism many were returned to their rightful owners, brought back from the brink and restored to their former glory.

9

Co, gdzie, kiedy
What, where, when

In this unit you will learn
- *how to ask what, where and when questions*
- *how to arrange a meeting*
- *how to describe a location*

In this unit you will learn how to ask specific questions about who, what, where, etc. and how to answer these questions by using descriptions of place and time.

Dialogue 1 **Dialog pierwszy**

Andrew is back at his hotel. He looks through a book about the collection in the Czartoryski Museum when his mobile rings. It's Maria.

Vocabulary **Słówka**

Form in the dialogue	Dictionary form	English translation
co słychać		*how are things?*
wszystko		*everything, all*
dla + genitive		*for, for the sake of*

dla ciebie	dla, ty	*for you*
interesującą wiadomość	interesujący, wiadomość (f.)	*an interesting piece of news*
spotkać się	spotykać się > spotkać się	*meet up*
w twoim hotelu	twój hotel	*at/in your hotel*
o której		*at what time*
o czwartej		*at four*

Andrew	Słucham.	*Hello.*
Maria	Dzień dobry panie Andrzeju. Mówi Maria.	*Good afternoon (Mr) Andrew. Maria speaking.*
Andrew	Dzień dobry pani Mario. Co słychać?	*Good afternoon (Ms) Maria. How are things?*
Maria	Wszystko dobrze, dziękuję. Mam interesującą wiadomość dla pana. Kiedy możemy się spotkać?	*Everything is fine, thanks. I've got an interesting (piece of) news for you. When can we meet?*
Andrew	Dzisiaj?	*Today?*
Maria	Dobrze.	*OK.*
Andrew	Gdzie?	*Where?*
Maria	W pana hotelu.	*At your hotel.*
Andrew	O której?	*What time?*
Maria	O czwartej.	*At four.*
Andrew	Dobrze. Do zobaczenia.	*OK. See you later.*
Maria	Do widzenia.	*Goodbye.*

Dialogue 2 Dialog drugi

Andrew arranges to meet Maria in the lounge of the Hotel Pod Różą where he's staying. The clock strikes four just as Maria walks into the hotel lounge.

Vocabulary **Słówka**

Form in the dialogue	Dictionary form	English translation
co się stało	stawać się > stać się	_what's happened_
fascynującą informację	fascynujący, informacja	_a fascinating bit of information_
jaką	jaki	_what, what sort of_
chodźmy	chodzić > pochodzić	_let's go_
wytłumaczę	tłumaczyć > wytłumaczyć, ty	_I'll explain to you_
po drodze	po, droga	_on the way_
dokąd		_where (to)_
niedaleko + gen.		_not far away (from)_
tuż obok + gen.		_right next door (to)_
obok Rynku		_next to the Market Square_
jesteśmy umówieni	umówiony; umawiać się > umówić się	_we've got an appointment/ arrange a meeting_
z Ewą	Ewa	_with Ewa_

Andrew	Co się stało?	_What's happened?_
Maria	Mam fascynującą informację dla pana.	_I've got a fascinating piece of information for you._
Andrew	Jaką informację?	_What sort of information?_
Maria	Chodźmy.	_Let's go._
	Wytłumaczę wszystko po drodze.	_I'll explain everything on the way._
Andrew	Dokąd idziemy?	_Where are we going?_
Maria	Niedaleko.	_Not far._
	Na ulicę Sienną.	_To Sienna Street._
	Tuż obok Rynku.	_Just next to the Market Square._
	Jesteśmy umówieni z Ewą.	_We're meeting Ewa._

Dialogue 3 **Dialog trzeci**

They walk along Floriańska Street to the Market Square. By St Mary's Church (**Kościół Mariacki**) they turn left into Sienna Street. Andrew is intrigued. He wants to know who Ewa is.

Vocabulary **Słówka**

Form in the dialogue	Dictionary form	English translation
przyjaciółka		*(female) friend*
pracuje	pracować > popracować	*she works*
archiwum		*archive(s)*
genealogiem	genealog	*genealogist*

Andrew	Kto to jest Ewa?	*Who's Ewa?*
Maria	Ewa to moja przyjaciółka.	*Ewa's my friend.*
	Pracuje w Archiwum.	*She works at the Archive(s).*
	Jest genealogiem.	*She's a genealogist.*

Dialogue 4 **Dialog czwarty**

Andrew and Maria get to the Archive(s) at a quarter past four.
Ewa's already waiting for them in the foyer. Maria introduces them.

Vocabulary **Słówka**

Form in the dialogue	Dictionary form	English translation
bardzo mi miło	bardzo, ja, miły	*pleased to meet you (it's very nice/welcome for me)*
do mojego biura	do, mój, biuro	*to my office*

Maria	Ewo, to jest pan Andrew Stewart.	*Ewa, this is Mr Andrew Stewart.*
Ewa	Dzień dobry panu.	*Good afternoon, sir.*
Andrew	Bardzo mi miło.	*Pleased to meet you.*
Ewa	Chodźmy do mojego biura.	*Let's go to my office.*

Dialogue 5 **Dialog piąty**

Ewa takes Maria and Andrew to her office on the second floor. They go
up an old wooden staircase. The stairs creak. The air's full of the aroma of
old books and papers.

Vocabulary Słówka

Form in the dialogue	Dictionary form	English translation
rozumiem	rozumieć > zrozumieć	I understand, I gather
szuka pan rodziny	szukać > poszukać, rodzina	you're looking for relatives/ family
moi przodkowie	mój, przodek	my ancestors, my forebears
pochodzą z + gen.	pochodzić >	come, originate from
mieszkali	mieszkać	lived
byli	być	they were
szuka + gen.	szukać > poszukać	is looking for

Ewa	Rozumiem, że szuka pan rodziny w Polsce.	*I understand (that) you're looking for (your) family in Poland.*
Andrew	Tak.	*Yes.*
	Wiem, że moi przodkowie pochodzą z Polski.	*I know that my ancestors come from Poland.*
Ewa	Pana przodkowie mieszkali w Polsce, ale byli Szkotami.	*Your ancestors lived in Poland but they were Scottish.*

Insight

We have already looked at how to remember words by association, but you can also build 'families' of words that are grouped by subject:

▶ nationalities, professions, family, shopping
▶ things you like/don't like, things you like doing/don't like doing
▶ masculine nouns, feminine nouns, neuter nouns
▶ nouns in genitive, nouns in accusative, etc.

It's a good way to revise what you have learned so far. Keep each 'family' of words in a separate envelope which is clearly marked so you can find it easily.

Let's practise

▶ Copy the dialogues (both the Polish and English parts) onto small pieces of paper.
▶ Mix the pieces and reconstruct the dialogues correctly (both parts).
▶ Mix the pieces again and reconstruct the Polish side of the dialogues.
▶ Separate the Polish and English parts of the dialogues. Turn the Polish parts face down and mix them again. Turn them face up at random and translate into English.
▶ Do the same exercise with the English parts of the dialogues.

How the language works

◀ℐ **CD2, TR 16**

Asking questions

Co (*what*), **kto** (*who*), **gdzie** (*where*) and **kiedy** (*when*) help us create open questions in Polish (questions which require a specific answer rather than a simple 'yes' or 'no'):

Co to jest?	*What is it?*
To jest **hotel**.	*It is a hotel.*
Kto to jest?	*Who is it?*
To jest **Anna**.	*This is Anna.*
Gdzie to jest?	*Where is it?*
To jest **w Krakowie**.	*It is in Kraków.*
Kiedy to jest?	*When is it?*
To jest **w piątek**.	*It is on Friday.*

Answering a question beginning with **gdzie** (*where*) will require giving a location, and grammatically speaking this usually means using a preposition (words like: *in, at, on, above,* etc.) with a case called the locative. You have come across nouns in the locative before in this course. They are usually accompanied by a small word called a preposition such as: **w** (*in*) or **na** (*on*):

w Polsce	*in Poland*
w Krakowie	*in Kraków*
w Anglii	*in England*
w sklepie	*in the shop*
w hotelu	*in a hotel*
w pokoju	*in a room*
w Archiwum	*in the Archives*
w muzeum	*in the museum*
na ulicy	*in the street*
na Rynku	*in the market square*
na uniwersytecie	*at the university*
na/po schodach	*on/down the stairs*
na parterze	*on the ground floor*

As you can see from the examples above, both **w** and **na** are used to describe the location. How do you know when to use **w** and when to use **na**?

Let's begin with **na**. It's best to learn these expressions by heart:

na ulicy	*in the street*
na placu (plac)	*in the square*
na Rynku	*in the Market Square*
na uniwersytecie	*at the university*
na poczcie (poczta)	*at the post office*
na dworcu (dworzec)	*at the rail/bus station*
na schodach	*on the stairs*
na balkonie (balkon)	*on the balcony*
na werandzie (weranda)	*on the verandah*
na tarasie (taras)	*on the terrace, patio*

Districts within towns use **na**:

na Starym Mieście	*in the Old Town*
na Mokotowie	*in Mokotów – a district of Warsaw*

Towns, cities, villages and countries use **w(e)**:

w Polsce	*in Poland*
we Francji	*in France*
w Anglii	*in England*
we Włoszech	*in Italy*
w Szkocji	*in Scotland*
w Niemczech	*in Germany*
w Ameryce	*in America*
w Kanadzie	*in Canada*
w Australii	*in Australia*
w Japonii	*in Japan*

Although this is not an exhaustive list it will give you a good start.

You may have spotted a curious discrepancy between Dialogue 2 and the list above. Why does Maria say: **Na ulicę (Sienną)** while the list above gives **na ulicy?**

This is because **na** can mean *on/in/at* as well as *to*. For example:

Idziemy na ulicę Sienną.	*We are going to Sienna Street.*
Mieszkamy na ulicy Siennej.	*We live in Sienna Street.*

▶ When **na** means *to*, the noun that follows is in the accusative case.
▶ When **na** means *on/in/at*, the noun is in the locative case.

You may also have noticed that **za** does not use the locative but the instrumental: **za domem**. Za leads a similar double life:

Idzie za dom. (accusative)	*S/he/it's going behind the house.*
Samochód stoi za domem. (instrumental)	*The car's (standing) behind the house.*

Answering a question beginning with **kiedy** (*when*) gives us an opportunity to look closer at the group of words and expressions related to time, or adverbials of time – to give them their proper grammatical name.

dzisiaj (or dziś)	today	nigdy	never
wczoraj	yesterday	rzadko	rarely
jutro	tomorrow	rano	in the morning
zaraz	in a moment	po południu	in the afternoon
później	later	wieczorem	in the evening
często	often	w nocy	at night
czasami	sometimes		

Vocative

So far you have become familiar with some Polish cases such as nominative, genitive, accusative or instrumental. But there is one case we haven't mentioned so far – the vocative. Vocative forms are used to address whoever we are speaking or writing to directly:

Basiu! Kasiu! Mario! Panie Andrzeju! Ewo!

Droga **Barbaro!**	*Dear Barbara!*
Kochana **Mamusiu!**	*Beloved Mum!*
Szanowni **Państwo!**	*Dear ladies and gentlemen!*
Ty **idioto!**	*You idiot!*
Ty **świnio!**	*You swine!*

Listen and repeat

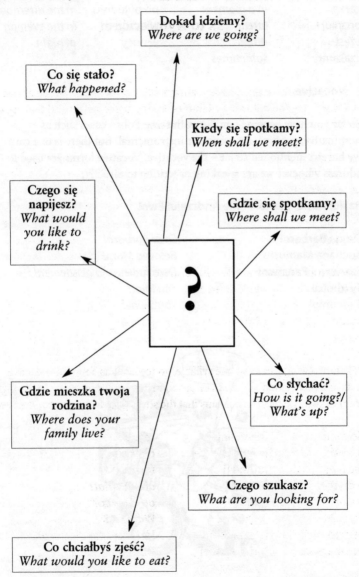

Dokąd idziemy?
Where are we going?

Co się stało?
What happened?

Kiedy się spotkamy?
When shall we meet?

Czego się napijesz?
What would you like to drink?

Gdzie się spotkamy?
Where shall we meet?

?

Gdzie mieszka twoja rodzina?
Where does your family live?

Co słychać?
How is it going?/ What's up?

Czego szukasz?
What are you looking for?

Co chciałbyś zjeść?
What would you like to eat?

Pronunciation guide **Jak to wymówić?**

Stress

Stress (emphasis, accent) almost always falls on the last syllable but one of a word. Try the following examples, taking them slowly and putting a gentle emphasis on the last syllable but one:

wy-<u>sta</u>-wa	*display*	cy-<u>try</u>-na	*lemon*
po-ma-<u>rań</u>-cza	*orange*	her-<u>ba</u>-ta	*tea*
ka-<u>wiar</u>-nia	*coffee shop*	<u>re</u>-laks	*relaxation*

Remember that the **kreska** (acute accent) ´ on the letter **ó** indicates that the pronunciation is [u]. It does not indicate stress or emphasis.

Listen to and repeat the following examples. Stress is indicated in the square brackets by a capital letter:

ogród	[Ogrut]	*garden*
pokój	[pOkuj]	*room*

When two words, each of one syllable, go together as a unit of meaning, such as a preposition and noun or pronoun, they are pronounced as a single word of two syllables. This means that the stress goes on the first of the two:

do mnie	[dOmnie]	*to me*
na nich	[nAnich]	*on them*
dla niej	[dlAniej]	*for her*
o czym?	[Oczym]	*about what?*
o kim?	[Okim]	*about who?*
Po co?	[pOco]	*What for?*
Jest po nim.	[jest pOnim]	*He's done for (finished).*
Nie ma za co.	[niEma zAco]/ [niemazAco]	*Don't mention it.*

Although stress in Polish is predictable and almost always falls on the penultimate syllable, there are some exceptions where stress falls on the third syllable from the end. Exceptions include words of Latin or Greek origin such as:

matematyka	[matem**A**tyka]	*mathematics*
fizyka	[f**I**zyka]	*physics*
gramatyka	[gram**A**tyka]	*grammar*
muzyka	[m**U**zyka]	*music*
biblioteka	[bib**li**O**teka]	*library*
informatyka	[inform**A**tyka]	*information technology*

Test yourself

Exercise 1

Translate the following sentences into Polish. (blue cards)

a Hello (on the phone).
b John speaking.
c How are things?
d Fine, thanks.
e I've got an interesting (piece of) news.
f See you later.
g When can we meet?
h Where can we meet?
i What happened?
j Where are we going?
k Let's go.
l Who is it?
m Who is Ewa?
n Ewa is my friend.
o Ewa works in the Archive(s).
p Ewa works in Kraków.

Exercise 2

Respond in Polish to the following statements and questions. Check your answers on the recording. (yellow cards)

a Dokąd idziemy?
(To Sienna Street.)

b O której spotkamy się?
(At four.)

c Do widzenia.
(See you later.)

d Gdzie jest ulica Sienna.
(Just next to the Market Square.)

e Kto to jest Ewa?
(Ewa is my friend.)

f Czy ma pan rodzinę w Polsce.
(I think so.)

g Pan przodkowie byli Szkotami.
(Really?)

Exercise 3

Complete the following sentences. (green cards)

a Co się _____ ?

b Wytłumaczę wszystko po _____ .

c Dokąd _____ ?

d Słucham? _____ Maria.

e Mam interesującą _____ dla pana.

f Kiedy _____ się?

g Ewa to moja _____ .

h Ewa pracuje w _____ .

Exercise 4

Fill in the table. Write as many items in each category as you can find from the course so far. (green cards)

Family members	Professions	Nationalities

Did you know? (purple cards)
Famous Poles

▶ Nicolaus Copernicus – Mikołaj Kopernik (1473–1543) – Father of modern astronomy. He was the first astronomer to formulate a modern heliocentric theory of the solar system.

▶ Maria Skłodowska – Curie (1867–1934) – Pioneer in the field of radioactivity. Discovered polonium and radium (used widely in cancer treatment). 1903 – Nobel prize winner (physics). 1911 – Nobel prize winner (chemistry).

▶ Joseph Conrad – Józef Teodor Konrad Korzeniowski (1857–1924) – Writer, author of *Lord Jim*, *The Heart of Darkness* (which was the inspiration for the classic Francis Ford Coppola's film *Apocalypse Now*), *Nostromo*, *The Secret Agent* and many more.

▶ Paweł Edmund Strzelecki – (Sir Paul Edmund de Strzelecki) (1797–1873) – Explorer and geologist, discovered the highest peak in Australia, which he named Mount Kościuszko. In 1846, awarded a Gold medal by the Royal Geographical Society; friend and supporter of Florence Nightingale.

▶ Jan Heweliusz (1611–87) – astronomer from Gdańsk, author of the first map of the Moon, member of the Royal Society. Invented the periscope.

▶ Tadeusz Kościuszko (1746 –1817) – Polish general, a leader of the 1794 uprising against the Russian Empire, a hero of American War of Independence.

- Ignacy Łukasiewicz (1822–82) – Father of the oil industry. In 1852 he invented the kerosene lamp. In 1854, he oversaw the drilling of the first oil well in the world near Jasło. The oil industry was born.
- Rudolf Modrzejewski – (Ralph Modjeski) (1861–1940) – The best constructor of bridges in the USA. His bridges included the Mississipi Bridge at Rock Island, Illinios and Manhattan Bridge in New York.
- Henryk Sienkiewicz (1846–1916) – Author of the famous novel *Quo Vadis* and 1905 Nobel prize winner for outstanding merit as an epic writer.
- Frederic Chopin (1810–49) – Composer.
- Antoni Norbert Patek (1811–77) – Polish cavalry officer who took part in the November Uprising of 1830 against the Russian Empire. After the defeat he emigrated to Switzerland where in 1839 he set up a watch-making firm. His business partner was Jean Adrienne Philippe. Together they have created one of the most prestigious watch brands in the world (Patek Philippe).
- John Paul II Karol Józef Wojtyła (1920–2005) – Archbishop of Kraków and later Pope of Rome.
- Lech Wałęsa (1943–) – the leader of 'Solidarity' and the first post communist President of Poland.

10

Mój dziadek był ...
My grandfather was ...

In this unit you will learn
- *how to talk about people in the past*
- *how to talk about events in the past*
- *how to describe what you saw and where you went in the past*

In this unit you'll learn how to talk about people and things in the past.

Dialogue 1 **Dialog pierwszy**

Maria, Andrew and Ewa are sitting in Ewa's elegant office. Ewa asks if Andrew has been to the Czartoryski Museum.

Vocabulary **Słówka**

Form in the dialogue	Dictionary form	English translation
był pan	być	*you have been*
byłem	być	*I went, I was*
wczoraj		*yesterday*
portret		*portrait*

Ewa	Czy był pan w Muzeum Czartoryskich?	*Have you been to (in) the Czartoryski Museum?*
Andrew	Tak, byłem wczoraj.	*Yes, I went (there) yesterday.*
Ewa	Czy widział pan portret swojego przodka?	*Did you see the portrait of your ancestor?*

Dialogue 2 Dialog drugi

Andrew is surprised by the news of his ancestor's portrait.

Vocabulary Słówka

Form in the dialogue	Dictionary form	English translation
słynny		*famous*
pułkownikiem	pułkownik	*colonel*
w służbie	służba	*in the service*
polskiego króla	polski król	*of the Polish king*
nazywał się	nazywać się > nazwać się	*his (sur)name was*

| Andrew | Mój przodek był słynny? | *Was my ancestor famous?* |
| Ewa | O tak. Nazywał się Robert Sutherland. Był pułkownikiem artylerii w służbie polskiego króla Jana Kazimierza. Jego portret jest w Muzeum Czartoryskich. | *Oh yes. His name was Robert Sutherland. He was a colonel of the artillery in the service of the Polish king, John Casimir. His portrait is at the Czartoryski Museum.* |

Dialogue 3 **Dialog trzeci**

Andrew can't quite believe his ears. To give him some time to get used to the idea, Ewa offers him and Maria a cup of tea.

Vocabulary **Słówka**

Form in the dialogue	Dictionary form	English translation
napijecie się + gen.	napić się	*you'll have a drink of, you'll have something to drink, have enough to drink*
herbaty	herbata	*(some) tea*
z + instrumental		*with*

z mlekiem	mleko	*with milk*
z cytryną	cytryna	*with lemon*
z cukrem	cukier	*with sugar*
proszę poczęstować się + instrumental	częstować się > poczęstować się	*please help yourself to*
herbatnikami	herbatnik	*(to) biscuits*

Ewa	Czy napijecie się herbaty?	*Would you like a cup of tea?*
Andrew	Tak, proszę.	*Yes, please.*
Ewa	Z mlekiem czy z cytryną?	*With milk or with lemon?*
Andrew	Z mlekiem proszę.	*With milk, please.*
Maria	Z cytryną i z cukrem proszę.	*With lemon and (some) sugar please.*
Ewa	Proszę poczęstować się herbatnikami.	*Please help yourself to (some) biscuits.*
Andrew	Dziękuję.	*Thank you.*

Dialogue 4 **Dialog czwarty**

Ewa shows Andrew and Maria various documents. Andrew is curious to hear if there are any of his relatives still in Poland.

Vocabulary **Słówka**

Form in the dialogue	Dictionary form	English translation
jakichś* krewnych	jakiś krewny	*any relatives*
pana daleka krewna	pan, daleki krewny	*a distant female relation*
znajdę	znajdować > znaleźć	*I'll find (it)*

*This form is normally pronounced as if written [jakiś], so don't worry about pronouncing the **ch** here.

Andrew	Czy mam jakichś krewnych w Polsce?	*Do I have any relatives in Poland?*
Ewa	Tak, pana daleka krewna mieszka w Krakowie.	*Yes, your distant (female) relative lives in Kraków.*
Andrew	Czy ma pani adres?	*Have you got the address?*
Ewa	Jeszcze nie, ale znajdę.	*Not yet, but I'll find it.*

Let's practise

▶ Copy the dialogues (both the Polish and English parts) onto small pieces of paper.

▶ Mix the pieces and reconstruct the dialogues correctly (both parts).

▶ Mix the pieces again and reconstruct the Polish side of the dialogues.

▶ Separate the Polish and English parts of the dialogues. Turn the Polish parts face down and mix them again. Turn them face up at random and translate into English.

▶ Do the same exercise with the English parts of the dialogues.

How the language works

Days of the week

poniedziałek	*Monday*
wtorek	*Tuesday*
środa	*Wednesday*
czwartek	*Thursday*
piątek	*Friday*
sobota	*Saturday*
niedziela	*Sunday*

In Polish the days of the week do not use an initial capital letter.

Now look at the following sentences, involving **wczoraj** (*yesterday*), **dziś** (*today*) and **jutro** (*tomorrow*).

Dziś jest poniedziałek.	*Today is Monday.*
Jutro będzie wtorek.	*Tomorrow will be Tuesday.*
Wczoraj była niedziela.	*Yesterday was Sunday.*
Dziś jest czwartek.	*Today is Thursday.*
Jutro będzie piątek.	*Tomorrow will be Friday.*
Wczoraj była środa.	*Yesterday was Wednesday.*
Dziś jest piątek.	*Today is Friday.*
Wczoraj był czwartek.	*Yesterday was Thursday.*
Jutro będzie sobota.	*Tomorrow will be Saturday.*

Did you notice that *was* is **była** with **niedziela** (*Sunday*) and **środa** (*Wednesday*), but **był** with **czwartek** (*Thursday*). This is because past tense verbs in Polish have forms to match the gender of their subject, i.e. there are separate endings for masculine, feminine and neuter.

◄) **CD2, TR 24**

The past

Let's look at the verb **być** (*to be*) in the past form:

	Masculine	*Feminine*	*Neuter*
ja	byłem	byłam	
ty	byłeś	byłaś	
on	był		
ona		była	
ono			było
my	byliśmy	byłyśmy	
wy	byliście	byłyście	
oni	byli		
one		były	

Now look at the past tense of the verb **mieć** (*to have*):

	Masculine	Feminine	Neuter
ja	miałem	miałam	
ty	miałeś	miałaś	
on	miał		
ona		miała	
ono			miało
my	mieliśmy	miałyśmy	
wy	mieliście	miałyście	
oni	mieli		
one		miały	

If you take a closer look at the past forms above you'll notice that there is a regular pattern.

▶ To form the past tense of regular verbs, remove the -ć of the infinitive (dictionary form), and add the following endings

Masculine (on)	Feminine (ona)	Neuter (ono)
-łem	-łam	
-łeś	-łaś	
-ł	-ła	-ło

Virile (males or mixed group of males and females)	Non-virile (females)
-liśmy	-łyśmy
-liście	-łyście
-li	-ły

▶ With verbs that have an infinitive ending in -eć, the e turns into a before the ł of the past tense suffix. Before l, the e remains.

Let's have a look at some examples of sentences in the past tense for **być**, **widzieć** and **kupić**:

Byłem wczoraj w muzeum.	*I was in the museum yesterday.* (male)
Widziałem obraz Leonarda da Vinci.	*I saw the painting by Leonardo da Vinci.* (male)
Kupiłem album o Krakowie.	*I bought a (coffee table) book about Kraków.* (male)
Byłam wczoraj w Amsterdamie.	*I was in Amsterdam yesterday.* (female)
Widziałam obraz Rembrandta.	*I saw a painting by Rembrandt.* (female)
Kupiłam zakładki.	*I bought some bookmarks.* (female)

◀》 **CD2, TR 25**

Listen and repeat

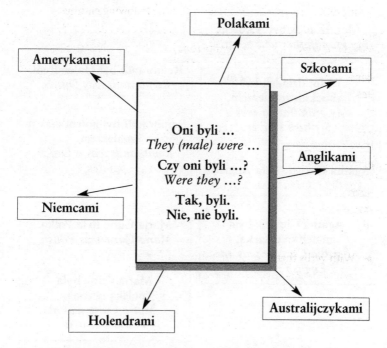

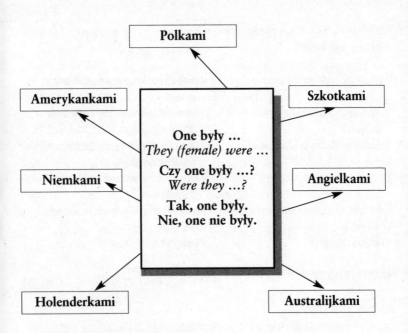

Polkami

Amerykankami

Szkotkami

One były …
They (female) were …

Czy one były …?
Were they …?

Tak, one były.
Nie, one nie były.

Niemkami

Angielkami

Holenderkami

Australijkami

Mój dziadek był Szkotem.
My grandfather was Scottish.

Mój dziadek był szkockim żołnierzem.
My grandfather was a Scottish soldier.

Rembrandt był Holendrem.
Rembrandt was Dutch.

Rembrandt był holenderskim malarzem.
Rembrandt was a Dutch painter.

Agatha Christie była Angielką.
Agatha Christie was English.

Agatha Christie była angielską pisarką.
Agatha Christie was an English writer.

Maria Curie była Polką.
Maria Curie was Polish.

Maria Curie była polską uczoną.
Maria Curie was a Polish scientist.

Insight

When learning a language on your own it's sometimes hard to keep yourself motivated. There's no tutor to praise you, and you don't always have an opportunity to use the language immediately. It's easy to forget how far you've come since the beginning of the course. One way to make yourself aware of how much you have already achieved is to keep an 'I can do … now' list. Keep adding to the list so it accurately reflects your efforts. You can use the headings from the unit title pages as prompts. For example:

▶ I can introduce myself.
▶ I can state my nationality and my profession.
▶ I can say I am or I am not tired/hungry, etc.

◀) CD2, TR 26

_____

Pronunciation guide **Jak to wymówić?**

Developing smoothness and fluency

Now that you have been introduced to the locative, there's the important matter of pronunciation to absorb if you want your Polish to be smooth and natural. It's important not to put a break between prepositions and what follows; you've already practised examples where a preposition takes the stress off what follows. Now pronounce the following combinations with prepositions slowly and smoothly. The most important point is that you should run the words together. Don't turn these one-consonant-letter prepositions into separate syllables. Remember that in the long term you'll build up fluency not by hurrying (and tripping) in the early stages, but by practising slowly and smoothly. Take things as slowly as you need to in order to keep them smooth; don't let anybody or anything rush you.

o + locative

o mnie	[Omnie]	*about me*
o Krzysztofie	[oksz …]	*about Krzysztof*
o Radomiu	[ora …]	*about Radom*

w + locative

w Internecie	[win ...]	*on the Internet*
w Kaziemierzu	[fk ...]	*in Kazimierz – a small town in Poland*
w Koszalinie	[fk ...]	*in Koszalin*
w Poznaniu	[fp ...]	*in Poznań*
w Samolocie	[fs ...]	*on the plane*
w Toruniu	[ft ...]	*in Toruń*

z + genitive

| z Bytomia | [zb ...] | *from Bytom* |
| z Okocimia | [zo ...] | *from Okocim* |

z + instrumental

| z psem | [sps ...] | *with a dog* |

Test yourself

Exercise 1

Work out the genders of the days of the week from their endings in the nominative.

- **a** poniedziałek
- **b** wtorek
- **c** środa
- **d** czwartek
- **e** piątek
- **f** sobota
- **g** niedziela

Exercise 2

Select the correct form of the verb from those given in brackets.
(green cards)

a Ewa (pracowała/pracował) w Archiwum.
b Andrew (kupił/kupiło) przewodnik po Krakowie.
c Mój mąż i ja (widzieliśmy/widziałyśmy) słynny obraz Leonarda.
d Adam i Andrew (były/byli) wczoraj w Krakowie.

Exercise 3

Translate the following sentences into Polish. (blue cards)

a Have you been to the Czartoryski Museum?
b Yes, I was there yesterday.
c Have you seen the painting by Leonardo?
d Your ancestor was Scottish.
e His name was Robert Sutherland.
f Would you like a cup of tea?
g Coffee with milk, please.
h Please help yourself to some biscuits.
i My distant relative lives in Poland.
j Have you got the address?
k Not yet.

Exercise 4

Complete the following sentences. (green cards)

a Herbata z mlekiem czy z _____?
b Pana daleka krewna _____ w Krakowie.
c Proszę poczęstować się _____.
d Widziałem portret mojego _____.
e Czy była pani w _____ Czartoryskich?
f Agatha Christie była angielską _____.
g Maria Skłodowska-Curie była _____.
h Rembrandt był holenderskim _____.

Exercise 5

Answer the following questions in Polish using the English prompts.
Check your answers and pronunciation on the recording. (yellow cards)

a Czy napijesz się herbaty?
(*Yes please, with milk.*)
b Czy był pan w Sukiennicach?
(*Not yet.*)
c Czy był pan na Wawelu?
(*Yes, I was there yesterday.*)
d Czy widział pan słynny obraz Leonarda?
(*Yes, it's fascinating.*)
e Kto to jest Robert Sutherland?
(*Robert Sutherland was my ancestor.*)
f Kim był Robert?
(*He was a colonel of artillery in the service of the Polish king.*)

Did you know? (purple cards)

The Husaria, the legendary Polish cavalry, were mounted on heavy and
swift horses. They were probably most famous for the wings attached to
the back of their armour, made on a wooden frame with vulture or eagle
feathers. Once in full charge the Husaria were almost unstoppable.

The Husarze (members of the Husaria regiment) were recruited from the
Polish nobility.

The most famous Husaria victories were at the Battle of Kircholm (1605)
against a much bigger Swedish army, at the Battle of Chocim (1673)
and at the Battle of Vienna (1683) against an overwhelming army of the
Ottoman Empire.

11

Nie wiedziałem, że oni byli …
I didn't know they were …

In this unit you will learn
- *how to say you didn't know/didn't think or didn't suppose something was the case*
- *how to describe different professions*
- *how to describe different nationalities*

In this unit you'll learn how to express that you didn't know, didn't think or didn't suppose something was the case. You'll also learn how to use plural forms of nationalities and professions.

Dialogue 1 **Dialog pierwszy**

Andrew and Maria have left Ewa's office and are walking slowly back to the hotel. Andrew's very surprised to hear that there were Scots living in Poland.

Vocabulary **Słówka**

Form in the dialogue	Dictionary form	English translation
wiedziałem	wiedzieć	*I knew*
także		*also*
Holendrzy	Holender	*Dutch people*

Anglicy	Anglik	*English people*
Niemcy	Niemiec	*Germans*
Żydzi	Żyd	*Jews*
Rosjanie	Rosjanin	*Russians*
Węgrzy	Węgr	*Hungarians*
Włosi	Włoch	*Italians*
Francuzi	Francuz	*French (people)*
robili	robić > zrobić	*were doing, were making*
kupcami	kupiec	*merchant*
złotnikami	złotnik	*goldsmith*
inżynierami	inżynier	*engineers*
tkaczami	tkacz	*weavers*
malarzami	malarz	*painters*
architektami	architekt	*architects*
żołnierzami	żołnierz	*soldiers*
ciekawe	ciekawy	*interesting*

Andrew	Nie wiedziałem, że Szkoci mieszkali w Polsce.	*I didn't know that Scots lived in Poland.*
Maria	Nie tylko Szkoci, ale także Holendrzy, Anglicy, Niemcy, Żydzi, Rosjanie, Węgrzy, Włosi i Francuzi.	*Not only Scots but also the Dutch, the English, Germans, Jews, Russians, Hungarians, Italians and the French.*
Andrew	Co robili w Polsce?	*What were they doing in Poland?*
Maria	Byli kupcami, złotnikami, inżynierami, tkaczami, malarzami, architektami i żołnierzami.	*They were merchants, goldsmiths, engineers, weavers, painters, architects and soldiers.*
Andrew	To bardzo ciekawe.	*That's very interesting.*

Dialogue 2 **Dialog drugi**

Maria asks about Andrew's family and what professions his relatives had.

Vocabulary **Słówka**

Form in the dialogue	Dictionary form	English translation
kim	kto	*what* (in terms of profession)
lekarzem	lekarz	*doctor*
stryj		*paternal uncle*
w artylerii	artyleria	*in the artillery*
w kawalerii	kawaleria	*in the cavalry*
przypuszczałem	przypuszczać > przypuścić	*suppose, think, imagine*
długa rodzinna tradycja	długi, rodzinny, tradycja	*long family tradition*

Maria	Kim był pana ojciec?	*What was your father? (What did your father do?)*
Andrew	Był lekarzem, ale mój stryj i mój dziadek byli żołnierzami. Stryj był w artylerii, a dziadek – w kawalerii. Nie przypuszczałem, że to taka długa, rodzinna tradycja.	*He was a doctor but my uncle and my grandfather were soldiers. My uncle was in the artillery, and my grandfather in the cavalry. I didn't think that it was such a long family tradition.*

Dialogue 3 **Dialog trzeci**

Andrew's curious as to what professions were common in Maria's family.

Vocabulary **Słówka**

Form in the dialogue	Dictionary form	English translation
kim pani była	kto, pani, być	*what were you, what did you do*
archiwistką pani mąż	archiwistka	*archivist (female) your husband*
dziennikarzem	dziennikarz	*journalist*
prawnikami	prawnik	*lawyers*
notariuszem	notariusz	*notary*
adwokatem	adwokat	*barrister*

Andrew	Kim pani była?	*What were you?*
Maria	Byłam archiwistką.	*I was an archivist.*
Andrew	A pani mąż?	*And your husband?*
Maria	Mój mąż był dziennikarzem.	*My husband was a journalist.*
Andrew	A pani ojciec?	*And your father?*
Maria	Mój ojciec i mój dziadek byli prawnikami. Dziadek był notariuszem, a ojciec – adwokatem.	*My father and my grandfather were lawyers. My grandfather was a notary, and my father a barrister.*

Let's practise

▶ Copy the dialogues (both the Polish and English parts) onto small pieces of paper.
▶ Mix the pieces and reconstruct the dialogues correctly (both parts).
▶ Mix the pieces again and reconstruct the Polish side of the dialogues.
▶ Separate the Polish and English parts of the dialogues. Turn the Polish parts face down and mix them again. Turn them face up at random and translate into English.
▶ Do the same exercise with the English parts of the dialogues.

How the language works

Plurals

In Unit 9 we started discussing plurals in Polish, although we mainly concentrated on masculine nouns. The dialogues in this unit give us an opportunity to look at plurals again.

Maria mentions many nationalities who lived in Poland in the past and the professions they had.

Nationality singular masculine	Nationality plural virile (males)	
Anglik	Anglicy	*English people*
Szkot	Szkoci	*Scottish people*
Niemiec	Niemcy	*Germans*
Rosjanin	Rosjanie	*Russians*
Holender	Holendrzy	*Dutch people*
Żyd	Żydzi	*Jews*
Węgier	Węgrzy	*Hungarians*
Włoch	Włosi	*Italians*
Francuz	Francuzi	*French people*

Singular	Plural	Instrumental plural	Example
żołnierz *(soldier)*	żołnierze	żołnierzami	Anglicy byli żołnierzami. *English were soldiers.*
inżynier *(engineer)*	inżynierowie	inżynierami	Holendrzy byli inżynierami. *Dutch were engineers.*
kupiec *(merchant)*	kupcy	kupcami	Żydzi byli kupcami. *Jews were merchants.*
złotnik *(goldsmith)*	złotnicy	złotnikami	Niemcy byli złotnikami. *Germans were goldsmiths.*
tkacz *(weaver)*	tkacze	tkaczami	Szkoci byli tkaczami. *Scots were weavers.*

malarz	malarze	malarzami	Włosi byli malarzami.
(painter)			*Italians were painters.*
architekt	architekci	architektami	Francuzi byli architektami.
(architect)			*French were architects.*

Listen and repeat

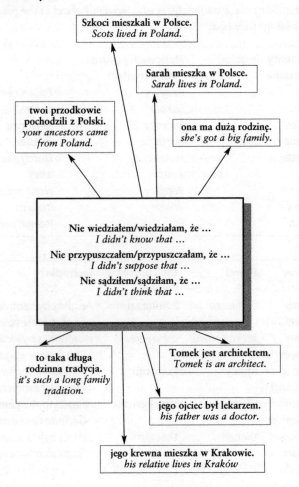

Szkoci mieszkali w Polsce.
Scots lived in Poland.

Sarah mieszka w Polsce.
Sarah lives in Poland.

twoi przodkowie pochodzili z Polski.
your ancestors came from Poland.

ona ma dużą rodzinę.
she's got a big family.

Nie wiedziałem/wiedziałam, że …
I didn't know that …
Nie przypuszczałem/przypuszczałam, że …
I didn't suppose that …
Nie sądziłem/sądziłam, że …
I didn't think that …

to taka długa rodzinna tradycja.
it's such a long family tradition.

Tomek jest architektem.
Tomek is an architect.

jego ojciec był lekarzem.
his father was a doctor.

jego krewna mieszka w Krakowie.
his relative lives in Kraków

Let's now look at how to form the plural of feminine nouns. Look at the following selection of nouns which have appeared so far in the course, and their plural forms:

Singular	English	Plural
książka	book	książki
zakładka	bookmark	zakładki
matka	mother	matki
córka	daughter	córki
taksówka	taxi	taksówki
widokówka	postcard (with a view)	widokówki
pocztówka	postcard	pocztówki
filiżanka	cup	filiżanki
żona	wife	żony
rodzina	family	rodziny
kobieta	woman	kobiety
herbata	tea	herbaty
koperta	envelope	koperty
karta	card/menu	karty
kawa	coffee	kawy
cytryna	lemon	cytryny
sprawa	matter	sprawy
godzina	hour	godziny
lampa	lamp	lampy
ulica	street	ulice
akademia	academy	akademie
kuchnia	kitchen/cuisine	kuchnie
fotografia	photograph	fotografie
droga	road	drogi

Hopefully, you can see a pattern emerging:

▶ Feminine nouns ending in -**ka** have the ending -**ki** in the plural. (Remember that in Polish **k** cannot be followed by **y** so it always is followed by **i**.)

▶ Nouns ending in -**ga** have the ending -**gi** in the plural (for a similar reason as above – **g** cannot be followed by **y** so it is always followed by **i**).

▶ Nouns ending in a consonant + **a** (i.e. **-ta**, **-wa**, **-na**, **-pa**, etc.) end in -y in the plural.

▶ Nouns ending in **-ia** have the ending -ie in the plural.

Although these rules do not apply to all feminine nouns, they will give you a very good start.

◄ **CD2, TR 32**

Pronunciation guide Jak to wymówić?

Intonation – the tune of a sentence

The most important thing to remember about Polish intonation is that statements in which your voice falls towards the end of a sentence can be turned into questions just by raising the pitch of your voice at the end.

Jest architektem.	(voice falling)	*He's an architect.*
Jest architektem?	(voice rising)	*Is he an architect?*

Spelling

Having different letters (or combination of letters) representing the same sound poses an obvious question: how do you know how to spell words containing these letters?

For example, if **ch** = **h** then when do you use one and not the other? **Ch** is a rule while **h** is an exception (there are fewer words spelled with **h** than with **ch** so in Poland children learn them by heart).

Similar rules applies to other letters:

Rule	Exception
ch	h
rz	ż
u	ó

How do you spell that? **Jak się to pisze?**

Proszę przeliterować *Please spell that*

Below are typical names used for spelling out loud. Being able to spell out loud is actually extremely useful in Poland, especially when Poles don't catch your non-Polish name, or if you're having trouble with a word they've used. You know now how to pronounce all the Polish names used in spelling out loud. The pronunciation of the letter name is given in square brackets after each letter.

A [a]   jak Adam
B [be]   jak Barbara
C [ce]   jak Celina (**c** is pronounced [ts] except before **i**, **h** and **z**)
D [de]   jak Dorota
E [e]   jak Ewa
F [ef]   jak Franciszek
G [gie]   jak Genowefa
H [cha]   jak Halina (**ch** single sound as in *loch*)
I [i]   jak Irena
J [jot]   jak Jan
K [ka]   jak Karol
L [el]   jak Leon
Ł [eł]   jak Łukasz (**ł** like an English *w*)
M [em]   jak Maria
N [en]   jak Natalia
O [o]   jak Olga
P [pe]   jak Piotr (no puff of air after **p**)
R [er]   jak Roman
S [es]   jak Stefan
T [te]   jak Tomasz
U [u]   jak Urszula
W [wu]   jak Wanda (**w** like an English *v*)
X [iks]   jak Xantypa (Ksantypa) (**x** isn't supposed to be a Polish
            letter, but is found in plenty of words like **fax**)

Y [igrek]	jak Ypsylon
Z [zet]	jak Zbigniew
Ż [żet]	jak Żaneta

The letters ą and ę can be described as **a** and **e z ogonkiem** (*with a little tail*). The final letters of the Polish alphabet are ź [ziet] or **zet z kreską** (*zed with an accent*) and ż [żet] or **z z kropką** (*zed with a dot*). The acute accent ′ is known as **kreska** in Polish, so ć, etc. can be described as **z kreską** (*with an accent*). Alternatively, find a short word starting or finishing with the letter you need:

ć [cie] jak ćma	**c** with an accent, as in the word for *moth*
ń [eń] jak koń	**n** with an accent, as in the word for *horse*
ó [u] jak ósemka	**o** with an accent, as in the word for *number eight*
ś [eś] jak śmiech	**s** with an accent, as in the word for *laughter*
ź [ziet] jak źródło	**z** with an accent, as in the word for *(water) spring* or *source*

Call **q** and **v** [ku] and [fał] if you need them. It's important to remember always to call **w** [wu], like the French *vous*.

Test yourself

Exercise 1

Practise forming plural endings on the following nouns. (green cards)

a kobieta (*woman*)
b doniczka (*flower pot*)
c pielęgniarka (*nurse*)
d przyjaciółka (*female friend*)
e kanapka (*sandwich*)
f marmolada (*marmalade*)
g reklama (*advertisement*)
h broszura (*leaflet*)

i kanapa (*sofa*)
j komoda (*chest of drawers*)
k sukienka (*dress*)

Exercise 2

Translate the following sentences into Polish. (blue cards)

a Scots lived in Poland.
b I didn't know English people lived in Poland.
c Not just English people, but French and Dutch as well.
d It's very interesting.
e What were you (what was your profession)?
f I was a doctor.
g And your mother?
h She was an archivist.
i And your father?
j My father was a barrister.
k My grandfather was a soldier.
l It's a family tradition.

◀) **CD2, TR 34**

Exercise 3

Follow the English prompts and answer the questions in Polish. You can hear the correct pronunciation on the recording. (yellow cards)

a Kim był twój dziadek?
(*He was a doctor.*)
b Czy Szkoci mieszkali w Polsce?
(*Yes, they were soldiers, merchants and weavers.*)
c Czym się zajmowali Włosi w Polsce?
(*Italians were architects and painters.*)
d Czym się zajmowali pani przodkowie?
(*They were lawyers.*)
e Czy oni są Rosjanami?
(*No, they are Germans.*)

Exercise 4

Complete the following sentences. (green cards)

a Maria była (archiwistką/archiwistka).
b Mój dziadek był (prawnikami/prawnikiem).
c Szkoci (mieszkał/mieszkali) w Polsce.
d To bardzo (ciekawy/ciekawe).
e Jego ojciec jest (prawnikiem/emerytką).
f Poproszę herbatę z (cytryna/cytryną).
g Pana przodek (byli/był) słynny.
h Chodźmy do mojego (biura/biuro).

Did you know? (purple cards)

▶ The classic sci-fi film *Solaris* is based on a story by the Polish writer Stanisław Lem.
▶ Science fiction literature has influenced Polish modern architecture and the 'Spodek' (*saucer*) in Katowice is a striking example of that trend. It's a concert hall and sports arena and it really does look like a giant flying saucer, especially at night.

12

***

Czy mogę ...?
Can I ...?

In this unit you will learn
- *how to ask if you can do something*
- *how to say what you can and cannot do*
- *how to say what you are and are not able to do*

In this unit you will learn how to ask for permission to do something and to express what you can and cannot do.

***

Dialogue 1 **Dialog pierwszy**

The following day Maria and Andrew are back in Ewa's office. Ewa's showing them some documents, old prints and drawings. Andrew would like to have a closer look.

Vocabulary **Słówka**

Form in the dialogue	Dictionary form	English translation
mogę	móc	*I can, I may*
obejrzeć	oglądać > obejrzeć	*(have a) look at*
co za		*what sort of*
mapa		*map*
wsi	wieś	*of a village*
otrzymał	otrzymywać > otrzymać	*he received*

od króla	król	*from the king*
duży majątek		*big estate, fortune*
niedaleko Krakowa		*near, not far from Kraków*
stary sztych		*an old print*
z widokiem	widok	*with a view*
dworu	dwór	*of the manor house*

◀) CD2, TR 35

Andrew	Czy mogę obejrzeć te dokumenty?	*Can I have a look at those documents, please?*
Ewa	Proszę bardzo.	*Certainly.*
Andrew	Co to za mapa?	*What sort of map is this?*
Ewa	To jest mapa wsi Nowe Szkoty.	*This is a map of a village (called) Nowe Szkoty.*
	Robert Sutherland otrzymał od króla duży majątek niedaleko Krakowa.	*Robert Sutherland received from the king a large estate not far from Kraków.*
	Zbudował tam dwór, a wieś nazwał Nowe Szkoty.	*He built a manor house there, and he called the village Nowe Szkoty.*
	Proszę. Tu jest stary sztych z widokiem dworu.	*Here you are. Here's an old print with a view of the manor.*

Dialogue 2 **Dialog drugi**

Andrew would like to know what happened to the manor house.

Vocabulary **Słówka**

Form in the dialogue	**Dictionary form**	**English translation**
niestety		*unfortunately*
prawie		*almost*
kompletnie	kompletny	*completely*

| zrujnowany | rujnować > zrujnować | *ruined, in ruins* |
| oczywiście | oczywisty | *certainly, obviously* |

Andrew	Co się stało z dworem?	*What happened to the manor house?*	◈ CD2. TR 36
Ewa	Niestety, dwór jest kompletnie zrujnowany.	*Unfortunately, the manor house is completely ruined.*	
Andrew	Czy mogę go zobaczyć?	*Can I see it?*	
Ewa	Oczywiście. Proszę, tu jest adres.	*Of course. Here's the address.*	

Dialogue 3 **Dialog trzeci**

Andrew wonders if Maria could take him to the manor house.

Vocabulary **Słówka**

Form in the dialogue	**Dictionary form**	**English translation**
pojechać	jechać > pojechać	*go (other than on foot)*
dziś		*today*
po południu		*in the afternoon, this afternoon*

Andrew	Czy może pani pojechać ze mną do Nowych Szkotów?	*Can you go with me (take me to) to Nowe Szkoty?*	◈ CD2. TR 37
Maria	Tak, oczywiście.	*Yes, of course.*	
Andrew	Czy możemy pojechać dziś po południu?	*Can we go this afternoon?*	
Maria	Dobrze.	*OK.*	

Let's practise

▶ Copy the dialogues (both the Polish and English parts) onto small pieces of paper.
▶ Mix the pieces and reconstruct the dialogues correctly (both parts).
▶ Mix the pieces again and reconstruct the Polish side of the dialogues.
▶ Separate the Polish and English parts of the dialogues. Turn the Polish parts face down and mix them again. Turn them face up at random and translate into English.
▶ Do the same exercise with the English parts of the dialogues.

Insight

Don't forget to read and listen to all the previous dialogues as well as the new ones from this unit. It's the best way of revising. Hopefully you have saved all the pieces of paper you have been copying the dialogues onto. See if you can reconstruct the Polish side of the story so far (from Unit 1). Practise reading the dialogues to improve your fluency.

How the language works

Adverbs

Adverbs are a very common group of words that are used in everyday language. They are 'relatives' of adjectives. While adjectives are natural companions to nouns, for example:

piękny rysunek	*a beautiful drawing*
dobry kucharz	*a good cook*

Adverbs are natural companions to verbs:

Pięknie rysuje.	*S/he draws beautifully.*
Dobrze gotuje.	*S/he cooks well.*

A lot of Polish adverbs are derived from adjectives, either by substituting -o for the adjective ending, or by modifying the end of the stem slightly and then adding -e. Here are some examples.

Adjective	Meaning	Adverb	Meaning
cichy	*quiet*	cicho	*quietly*
dokładny	*precise*	dokładnie	*precisely*
głupi	*stupid*	głupio	*stupidly*
piękny	*beautiful*	pięknie	*beautifully*
podobny	*similar*	podobnie	*similarly*
		podobno	*apparently*
prawdopodobny	*probable*	prawdopodobnie	*probably*
serdeczny	*warm, kind*	serdecznie	*cordially*

Some of these adverb forms are used to say how things are, in general:

Jest pięknie.	*It's beautiful.*
Jest ciepło/słonecznie.	*It's warm/sunny.*

Here are some more examples of adverbs in use:

Zimno mi.	*I'm cold. (Don't say **Jestem zimny/zimna** unless you want to say that you're a cold or frigid person.)*
Ciepło nam.	*We're warm.*
Chłodno.	*It's chilly.*
Trudno powiedzieć.	*It's difficult to say.*
oczywiście	*certainly*
dobrze	*OK, fine*

Asking permission

In Unit 8 you learnt the phrase **Czy można …?** as a way of asking permission. In this unit there is a more personal, individual way of asking if something is possible to do.

Singular		Plural	
ja mogę	*I can*	my możemy	*we can*
ty możesz	*you can*	wy możecie	*you can*
on może	*he can*	oni mogą	*they can* (males or mixed group)
ona może	*she can*	one mogą	*they* (females) *can*
ono może	*it can*	państwo mogą	*ladies and gentlemen can*
pan może	*sir can*		
pani może	*madam can*		

Let's look at some examples:

Czy mogę wejść?	*Can I come in?*
Czy możemy wyjść o piątej?	*Can we leave at five?*
Czy mogę obejrzeć fotografie?	*Can I have a look at the photos?*
Oni mogą zwiedzić Wawel dzisiaj.	*They can see Wawel today.*
Pani może kupić znaczki w kiosku.	*Madam can buy stamps at the kiosk.*

Mogę is used when asking for permission or when describing a readiness to do something. It's also the word you need for the purely physical ability to do something.

Nie mógł mówić, bo był u dentysty.	*He couldn't talk, because he'd been to the dentist's.*

If you want to describe the ability or know-how to do something you need to use the word **umiem**:

Umiem mówić po polsku.	*I can (know how to) speak Polish.*
Umiem prowadzić samochód.	*I can drive.*
Umiem gotować.	*I can cook.*

Let's take a look at all the forms of **umiem**.

◄)) CD2, TR 38

Listen and repeat

ja umiem *I am able to*	Umiem dobrze gotować. *I'm able to cook well.*
ty umiesz *you are able to*	Umiesz dobrze gotować. *You are able to cook well.*
on umie *he is able to*	On umie dobrze gotować. *He is able to cook well.*
ona umie *she is able to*	Ona umie dobrze gotować. *She is able to cook well.*
ono umie *it is able to*	Ono umie dobrze gotować. *It is able to cook well.*
pan/pani umie *sir/madam is able to*	Pan/pani umie dobrze gotować. *Sir/madam is able to cook well.*
my umiemy *we are able to*	Umiemy dobrze gotować. *We are able to cook well.*
wy umiecie *you are able to*	Umiecie dobrze gotować. *You are able to cook well.*
oni/one umieją *they are able to*	Oni/one umieją dobrze gotować. *They are able to cook well.*
państwo umieją *ladies and gentlemen are able to*	Państwo umieją dobrze gotować. *Ladies and gentlemen are able to cook well.*

Listen and repeat

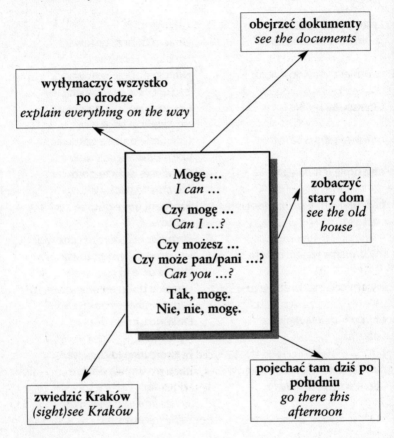

obejrzeć dokumenty
see the documents

**wytłymaczyć wszystko
po drodze**
explain everything on the way

Mogę ...
I can ...

Czy mogę ...
Can I ...?

Czy możesz ...
Czy może pan/pani ...?
Can you ...?

Tak, mogę.
Nie, nie, mogę.

**zobaczyć
stary dom**
*see the old
house*

zwiedzić Kraków
(sight)see Kraków

**pojechać tam dziś po
południu**
*go there this
afternoon*

It's useful to know that some Polish verbs don't need a translation for English *can*.

Nic nie słyszę.	*I can't hear anything.*
Co widzisz?	*What can you see?*

Pronunciation guide **Jak to wymówić?**

Abbreviations

When reading abbreviations in Polish such as **PKP Polskie Koleje Państwowe** (*Polish State Railways*), stress the last letter [pe ka p**E**].

Listen and repeat:

PWN Polskie Wydawnictwo Naukowe [pe wu e**N**]	*Polish Scientific Publishing*
UE Unia Europejska [u-**E**]	*the European Union*
itd. i tak dalej [i te d**E**]	*etc.*
TVP Telewizja Polska [tefaup**E**]	*Polish Broadcasting Company*
TVN [te fał e**N**]	*Polish commercial tv channel*
USA [u es **A**]	*USA*
SMS [es em e**S**]	*mobile phone texting system*
RP Rzeczpospolita Polska [er p**E**]	*Republic of Poland*
BMW [be em w**U**]	*BMW*

A few abbreviations are pronounced in a way that mimics the English rather than the Polish letter names, although you still need to stress the final syllables as you would if the letters had their Polish names:

CD [si d**I**] (Please note: **si** is pronounced as **s** + **i** and not as Polish **ś**.)
BBC [bi bi s**I**]
DVD [di wi d**I**]

Test yourself

Exercise 1

Translate the following sentences into Polish. (blue cards)

  a Can I have a look at the photographs, please?
  b This is a map of Kraków.
  c This is the photograph of the manor house.
  d Robert Sutherland received a large estate from the king.
  e Can I see the manor house?
  f Unfortunately the manor house is completely ruined.
  g Can you go with me (take me to), please?
  h Can we go there this afternoon?
  i Yes, of course.

◀) **CD2, TR 41**

Exercise 2

Respond in Polish to the following English prompts. (yellow cards)

  a Czy mogę obejrzeć te dokumenty?
    (*Yes, of course.*)
  b Co to jest?
    (*This is an old print with the view of the manor house.*)
  c Co się stało z dworem.
    (*My female relative lives there.*)
  d Czy mogę go zobaczyć?
    (*OK.*)
  e Czy możemy pojechać do Nowych Szkotów?
    (*Unfortunately, we can't.*)
  f Czy możemy zwiedzić Wawel dziś po południu?
    (*Yes, certainly.*)

Exercise 3

Complete the following sentences. (green cards)

a Chciałabym kupić _____ (*a book*).
b Czy można zapłacić _____ (*with a credit card*)?
c Co się stało z _____ (*manor house*)?
d Robert otrzymał duży _____ (*estate*) od króla.
e Lubię _____ (*paintings*) Leonarda i Rembrandta.
f Mój dziadek _____ (*built*) piękny dwór niedaleko Krakowa.
g Trzeba pojechać _____ (*by bus*).

Did you know? (purple cards)
Scots in Poland

Over the centuries, Polish immigrants settled all over the world. After World War II, a large group of Polish soldiers settled in the UK, America, Canada and Australia. This group was extended by a new wave of immigrants leaving Communist Poland in the 1980s. Since 2004, when Poland joined the European Union, hundreds of thousands of Poles have arrived in the UK. It's easy to forget that in the past there was an opposite trend, and Poland was the destination favoured by many thousands of Scottish immigrants. In the sixteenth and seventeenth centuries Scots were escaping religious persecution and poverty. They were merchants, weavers, doctors and soldiers. Scots settled around Gdańsk, Warsaw, Lublin and close to the Lithuanian border. Many of them served in the Polish Army as mercenaries. Henryk Sienkiewicz immortalized them in a character in his novel *Pan Wołodyjowski*: Hassling Kettling of Elgar was a fictional Colonel of Artillery in the service of King Jan Kazimierz. Scots assimilated very quickly in Polish society and many of their surnames were quickly Polonized: Forsyth became Forsycki, Cambell – Kamelski, Learmonth – Lermontow or Lermontowski, Gray – Grajewski.

Polish and Scottish aristocracies were also related through marriage. The mother of Charles Edward Stewart, better known as Bonnie Prince Charlie was also Polish: Maria Klementyna Sobieska was a granddaughter of the King of Poland Jan III Sobieski.

13

Jak dojechać do ...?
How do we get to ...?

In this unit you will learn
- *how to give and understand directions*
- *how to describe how far away places are*
- *how to describe geographical directions (east, west, etc.)*

In this unit you will learn how to give and understand directions.

Dialogue 1 **Dialog pierwszy**

After lunch, Andrew and Maria set off on the short journey to the manor house. It's a warm and sunny afternoon. They leave Kraków behind and drive through the countryside. Andrew would like to know how far the village of Nowe Szkoty is from Kraków.

Vocabulary **Słówka**

Form in the dialogue	Dictionary form	English translation
jak daleko	jak, daleko	*how far away*
od Krakowa		*from Kraków*
kiedyś		*ever, at any time, one day*
wiele lat	wiele, rok	*many years ago*

Andrew	Jak daleko są Nowe Szkoty?	*How far is it to Nowe Szkoty?*
Maria	Niedaleko, dwadzieścia kilometrów na zachód od Krakowa.	*Not far, 20 kilometres west of Kraków.*
Andrew	Czy była pani tam kiedyś?	*Have you ever been there?*
Maria	Tak, wiele lat temu.	*Yes, many years ago.*

Dialogue 2 **Dialog drugi**

Suddenly they come to a halt. There's been an accident and the road is closed. Maria asks a policeman what has happened.

Vocabulary **Słówka**

Form in the dialogue	Dictionary form	English translation
wypadek		*accident*
droga		*way, path, road*
zamknięta	zamknięty; zamykać > zamknąć	*closed*
zawrócić	zawracać > zawrócić	*turn round, turn back*
pojechać drogą na + acc.		*take the road to*

Maria	Przepraszam, co się stało?	*Excuse me, what happened?*
Policjant	Wypadek.	*An accident.*
	Droga jest zamknięta.	*The road's closed.*
	Dokąd państwo jadą?	*Where are you going?*
Maria	Do Nowych Szkotów.	*To Nowe Szkoty.*
Policjant	To muszą państwo zawrócić i pojechać drogą na Tarnów.	*Well, you have to turn round and take the road towards Tarnów.*
Maria	Dobrze. Dziękuję.	*OK. Thank you.*

Dialogue 3 **Dialog trzeci**

Maria and Andrew turn round and follow the road towards Tarnów for a while. After half an hour they reach Nowe Szkoty. Maria's not sure how to get to the old manor house. She stops the car and asks a lady who is passing by.

Vocabulary **Słówka**

Form in the dialogue	Dictionary form	English translation
dojechać do + gen.	dojeżdżać > dojechać	*get to, come up to, reach*
do starego dworu	do, stary, dwór	*to the old manor house*
trzeba		*you have to, one must, one needs to*
prosto	prosty	*straight (on)*
aż do kościoła	kościół	*right as far as the church*
skręcić w prawo	skręcać > skręcić	*turn right*
do małego skrzyżowania	mały, skrzyżowanie	*up to a small crossroads*
przy figurce	przy, figurka	*by a small statue*
w lewo		*left*
ta droga		*that road, the path*
prowadzi do	prowadzić > poprowadzić	*leads, takes you to*
nie ma za co		*not at all, no problem, don't mention it, it's OK*

◀ CD2, TR 44

Maria	Przepraszam panią, jak dojechać do starego dworu?	*Excuse me, how to get to the old manor house?*
Kobieta	Trzeba jechać prosto aż do kościoła.	*You need to go straight ahead as far as the church.*
	Koło kościoła proszę skręcić w prawo i jechać do	*By the church please turn right and go until a small*

	małego skrzyżowania przy figurce.	*crossroads by a statue.*
	Tam proszę skręcić w lewo.	*There, turn left, please.*
	Ta droga prowadzi do starego dworu.	*That road leads to the old manor house.*
Maria	Prosto, do kościoła, w prawo, przy figurce w lewo.	*Straight ahead, to the church, turn right, by the statue turn left.*
Kobieta	Tak.	*Yes.*
Maria	Dobrze. Dziękuję pani bardzo.	*OK. Thank you very much.*
Kobieta	Nie ma za co.	*Not at all.*

Let's practise

▶ Copy the dialogues (both the Polish and English parts) onto small pieces of paper.
▶ Mix the pieces and reconstruct the dialogues correctly (both parts).
▶ Mix the pieces again and reconstruct the Polish side of the dialogues.
▶ Separate the Polish and English parts of the dialogues. Turn the Polish parts face down and mix them again. Turn them face up at random and translate into English.
▶ Do the same exercise with the English parts of the dialogues.

◀ CD2, TR 45

Listen and repeat

Insight

To make it easier to give and understand directions you can make a simple map of Nowe Szkoty. Mark all the landmarks and how to get to the manor house. You can also make a similar map of the area where you live. Mark the landmarks and imagine yourself giving directions to your Polish guest.

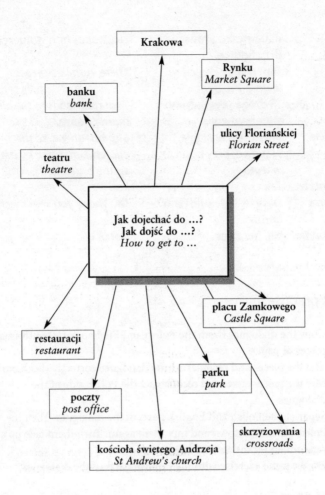

Krakowa

Rynku
Market Square

banku
bank

ulicy Floriańskiej
Florian Street

teatru
theatre

Jak dojechać do ...?
Jak dojść do ...?
How to get to ...

placu Zamkowego
Castle Square

restauracji
restaurant

parku
park

poczty
post office

skrzyżowania
crossroads

kościoła świętego Andrzeja
St Andrew's church

How the language works

◆) CD2, TR 46

Directions

Talking about distance and directions gives us another opportunity to
use more adverbials such as:

daleko	*far*
niedaleko	*not far*
blisko	*near*
prosto	*straight on*
w/na prawo	*to/on the right*
w/na lewo	*to/on the left*

You may also find using geographical directions useful:

północ *north*
na północy Polski
in the north of Poland

zachód *west*
na zachodzie Polski
in the west of Poland

wschód *east*
na wschodzie Polski
in the east of Poland

południe *south*
na południu Polski
in the south of Poland

Please note the following:

▶ **Północ** and **południe** also mean *midnight* and *noon* respectively.
▶ **Wschód** and **zachód** also mean *sunrise* and *sunset* respectively.

Maria describes Nowe Szkoty as being **dwadzieścia kilometrów na zachód od Krakowa** (*20 km west of Kraków*).

Let's practise describing various places in relation to other places.

Listen and repeat

Windsor jest 21 mil na zachód od Londynu.	*Windsor is 21 miles west of London.*
Felixstowe jest 15 mil na wschód od Ipswich.	*Felixstowe is 15 miles east of Ipswich.*

| Żelazowa Wola jest 60 kilometrów na zachód od Warszawy. | *Żelazowa Wola is 60 km west of Warsaw.* |
| Zakopane jest 100 kilometrów na południe od Krakowa. | *Zakopane is 100 km south of Kraków.* |

Imperfective vs. perfective verbs or why do Polish verbs go around in pairs?

iść > pójść
umawiać się > umówić się
siadać > usiąść
mówić > powiedzieć
pisać > napisać
jeść > zjeść

The short answer is for the same reason that in English there are different aspects of each tense – to reflect the difference between actions that have been completed, summed up, rounded off, taken as a whole and actions which are going on at a particular moment, or are repeated in a particular period. Let's look at some examples:

Oglądałem film cały wieczór.	*I was watching a film all evening.*
Obejrzałem film.	*I watched the film./I've watched the film.*
Jadłem śniadanie przy stole.	*I was eating breakfast at the table.*
Zjadłem śniadanie przy stole.	*I ate breakfast at the table.*
Pisałem często listy do mojej matki.	*I was often writing letters to my mother.*
Napisałem list do mojej matki.	*I wrote a letter to my mother.*

The partner in the pair that describes ongoing actions is called 'imperfective' while the form which describes completed or packaged actions is called 'perfective'. Whereas English usually uses extra elements (*-ing*, *-en*, etc.) to make these distinctions, Polish uses different verbs, which is why Polish verbs in vocabularies and dictionaries mostly go around in pairs. For an imperfective verb the fact the action is ongoing is important. For perfective verbs the completion of the action is more important.

In the examples above:

- ▶ **Oglądałem (oglądać)** is imperfective   *I was watching*
- ▶ **Obejrzałem (obejrzeć)** is perfective.   *I watched*
- ▶ **Jadłem (jeść)** is imperfective.   *I was eating*
- ▶ **Zjadłem (zjeść)** is perfective.   *I ate*
- ▶ **Pisałem (pisać)** is imperfective.   *I was writing*
- ▶ **Napisałem (napisać)** is perfective.   *I wrote*

This is the reason why in the glossaries accompanying the dialogues you often see two Polish versions of the same English verb. This book also systematically puts imperfective verbs first and perfective second (which is what most books do), and backs this up with a little arrowhead pointing away from the imperfective verb and towards the perfective.

Insight

It may help if you think of the arrowhead as a channel or funnel, packaging the wide-open action of the imperfective verb into the summed-up or completed perfective verb.

People find images useful in thinking about aspect. The one most people find useful is that an imperfective verb films or videos an action going on, whereas a perfective takes a single photo of it. As you look at more examples, perhaps other images of your own will occur to you. Images are good, because they get you away from English, which has its own quite different ways of doing things grammatically.

Let's go through some examples of perfective and imperfective verbs you have come across in the course so far.

Verbs: imperfective > perfective	English translation	Example
siedzieć > posiedzieć	*to sit, stay*	Siedzę w domu. *I'm (sitting) at home.* Niech pan jeszcze posiedzi. *Stay a bit longer.*

Verbs: imperfective > perfective	English translation	Example
siadać > usiąść	to sit down	Proszę usiąść. *Please sit down.* Siadają do stolu. *They're sitting down to the table./They're taking their seats at the table.*
pisać > napisać	to write	Piszę list. *I'm writing a letter.* Muszę napisać list. *I have to write a letter.*
czytać > przeczytać	to read	Czytam książkę o Krakowie. *I'm reading a book about Kraków.* Chciałabym przeczytać książkę o Krakowie. *I'd like to read a book about Kraków.*
wracać > wrócić	come/go back to, return	Kiedy wracasz do Polski? *When are you returning to Poland?* Chciałabym wrócić do Polski. *I'd like to return to Poland.*
dzwonić > zadzwonić	ring, telephone	Dzwonię do domu co tydzień. *I phone home every week.* Muszę zadzwonić do domu. *I have to phone home.*
zwiedzać > zwiedzić	go sightseeing, visit	Tysiące turystów zwiedza Wawel. *Thousands of tourists visit Wawel.*

Verbs: imperfective > perfective	English translation	Example
		Chciałbym zwiedzić Wawel.
		I would like to visit Wawel.
mówić > powiedzieć	*to speak*	Czy mówisz po polsku?
		Do you speak Polish?
		Powiedział coś po polsku.
		He said something in Polish.
płacić > zapłacić	*to pay*	Ile płacę?
		How much (am I paying)?
		Chciałbym zapłacić rachunek.
		I'd like to pay the bill.
kupować > kupić	*to buy*	Kupuję gazetę codziennie.
		I'm buying a newspaper daily.
		Muszę kupić bilet.
		I have to buy a ticket.
widzieć > zobaczyć	*to see*	Nie widzę go.
		I can't see him.
		Zobaczyłam go w tłumie.
		I saw him in the crowd.

There is one more important thing you need to know about perfective verbs: they don't have a present tense – you need to use an imperfective verb for that.

We will return to perfective and imperfective forms in Unit 15 when you will find out why the knowledge of different verb forms is important for the future tense.

Pronunciation guide Jak to wymówić?

Words with double consonants

There is a group of words in Polish which, just like in English, have a double consonant in them: **hobby, Joanna, Anna, ghetto**. When pronouncing these words remember that a double letter = double pronunciation by repeating or prolonging the consonant:

hobby	[ho **b-b** i]	*hobby*
Joanna	[joa **n-n** a]	*Joanna*
Anna	[a **n-n** a]	*Anna*
lekki	[le **k-k** i]	*light*
Jagiełło	[jagie **ł-ł** o]	*Jagiełło* (name of Polish king dynasty)
wanna	[wa **n-n** a]	*bath*
getto	[ge **t-t** o]	*ghetto*

Test yourself

Exercise 1

Translate the following sentences into Polish. (blue cards)

a How far is Kraków?
b Not far.
c Have you ever been there?
d Yes, many years ago.
e Excuse me, what happened?
f An accident.
g You need to turn round.
h How to get to the village?
i Where are you going?
j Please turn right by the church.

k The road leads to the old manor house.
l The road is closed.

Exercise 2

Complete the following sentences. (green cards)

a Droga jest _____.
b Przepraszam, co się _____?
c Trzeba jechać _____ aż do kościoła.
d Koło figurki trzeba _____ w lewo.
e Droga jest zamknięta, musi pan _____.
f Nowe Szkoty są dwadzieścia kilometrów na _____ od Krakowa.
g Czy była pani tam _____?

🔊 **CD2, TR 48**

Exercise 3

Use the English prompts to answer the following questions in Polish.
Don't forget to check your answers on the recording. (yellow cards)

a Jak daleko jest Kraków?
(*Not far.*)
b Czy był pan kiedyś w Londynie?
(*No, but I would like to go there.*)
c Przepraszam, co się stało?
(*An accident.*)
d Dokąd jedziemy?
(*To Nowe Szkoty.*)
e Dokąd prowadzi ta droga?
(*To the old manor house.*)
f Gdzie trzeba skręcić?
(*Next to the church.*)

Did you know? (purple cards)
Figurki, kapliczki i krzyże (*religious statues, chapels and crosses*)

The Polish countryside is dotted with thousands of small statues, tiny chapels and wooden and iron crosses, which are an integral part of Polish heritage. They have been erected by private individuals, communities and public bodies for a large variety of reasons: to express gratitude, to commemorate an event, for prayer, etc. They were also used as landmarks and distance markers (just like in the dialogue above). They come in many different shapes and sizes: statues, crosses, and monuments often with a little figure of Virgin Mary, Jesus Christ or other saints inside. A wooden figure of Jesus is often shown sitting, lost in his thoughts, with his head supported on his hand. Traditionally this type of figure is called **Chrystus Frasobliwy** (Sorrowing Christ).

14

Jaki piękny ogród za domem
What a beautiful garden behind the house

In this unit you will learn
- *how to express appreciation*
- *how to describe a house and its contents*
- *how to describe what is around the house*

In this unit you will learn how to express your appreciation as well as how to describe a house and its surroundings. You will look at using numerals in Polish.

Dialogue 1 **Dialog pierwszy**

Maria and Andrew are following the directions to the old manor house. As they drive along a narrow winding country road they reach the top of the hill. From here you can see the sweeping view of the surrounding hills and the manor house in the valley. Andrew can't resist proclaiming how beautiful the view is.

Form in the dialogue	English translation
jaki	*what kind of, what a*
piękny widok	*beautiful, fine view*
stąd	*from here*
widać + acc.	*can be seen*

◀)) CD2, TR 49

Andrew	Jaki piękny widok!	*What a beautiful view!*
Maria	Tak, bardzo piękny. Stąd bardzo dobrze widać dwór.	*Yes, it's very beautiful. You can see the manor very well from here.*

Dialogue 2 **Dialog drugi**

Maria and Andrew have reached the house. They turn into the drive, go through the broken gate and stop in front of the manor house. They get out of the car and start wandering around. Maria takes a piece of paper out of her handbag. It's a description of the manor house copied from the old documents.

Vocabulary Słówka

Form in the dialogue	Dictionary form	English translation
był kiedyś		used to be, was once
salon		sitting room
sześć sypialni	sypialnia	six bedrooms
jadalnię	jadalnia	dining room
dwa pokoje gościnne	pokój gościnny	guest room
bibliotekę	biblioteka	library
kuchnię	kuchnia	kitchen, cuisine
spiżarnię	spiżarnia	larder, pantry
trzy łazienki	łazienka	three bathrooms
wygląda, że	wyglądać	it looks as if
ogród		garden
park		park
za + acc.		(moving) behind
za + instr.		(located) behind
za domem	dom	behind the house
mała kaplica	mały, kaplica	a small chapel
na prawo od		on/to the right of
od domu	dom	from the house
stajnie	stajnia	stables
szkoda, że		it's a pity (that)
chodźmy do środka	chodzić, środek	let's go in(side)
klucz		key
drzwi		doors
otwarte	otwarty	open

Andrew	To był kiedyś bardzo piękny dom.	*It was a very beautiful house once.*
Maria	Tak.	*Yes.*
	Miał salon, jadalnię, sześć sypialni, bibliotekę, dwa pokoje gościnne, kuchnię, spiżarnię, i trzy łazienki.	*It had a sitting room, a dining room, six bedrooms, a library, two guest rooms, a kitchen, a pantry, and three bathrooms.*

Andrew	Wygląda, że dom miał też piękny ogród i park.	*It looks like the house had also a beautiful garden and a park.*
Maria	Tak.	*Yes.*
	Ogród był za domem.	*The garden was behind the house.*
	W parku stała mała kaplica.	*In the park stood a small chapel.*
	Na prawo od domu były stajnie.	*On the right of the house there were stables.*
	Szkoda, że dom jest taki zrujnowany.	*It's a pity the house is so ruined.*
Andrew	Chodźmy do środka.	*Let's go inside.*
Maria	Czy ma pan klucz?	*Have you got the key?*
Andrew	Nie, ale drzwi są otwarte.	*No, but the door is open.*

Let's practise

Complete the dialogue practice exercise – you'll find instructions on how to do this in the 'Let's practise' section in Unit 13.

◀ CD2, TR 51

Listen and repeat

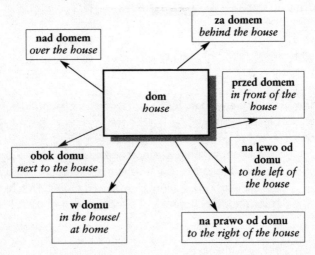

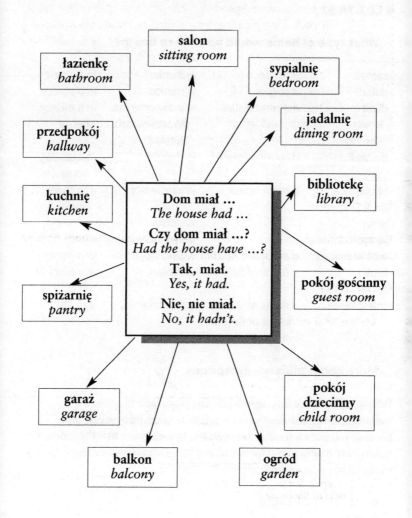

What's in the house?

salon	*sitting room*
łazienkę	*bathroom*
sypialnię	*bedroom*
przedpokój	*hallway*
jadalnię	*dining room*
kuchnię	*kitchen*
bibliotekę	*library*
spiżarnię	*pantry*
pokój gościnny	*guest room*
garaż	*garage*
pokój dziecinny	*child room*
balkon	*balcony*
ogród	*garden*

Dom miał …
The house had …

Czy dom miał …?
Had the house have …?

Tak, miał.
Yes, it had.

Nie, nie miał.
No, it hadn't.

How the language works

What type of home would you like to live in?

zamek	*a castle*	w zamku	*in a castle*
pałac	*a palace*	w pałacu	*in a palace*
dwór	*a manor house*	w(e) dworze (na dworze means 'outside')	*in a manor house*
dworek	*a country house*	w dworku	*in a country house*
kamienica	*a town house*	w kamienicy	*in a town house*
dom jednorodzinny/ wolno stojący	*a detached house*	w domu jednorodzinnym/ wolno stojącym	*in a house*
blok	*a block of flats*	w bloku	*in a block of flats*
mieszkanie	*a flat* (either in a block of flats or in a town house)	w mieszkaniu	*in a flat*

More about plurals – exceptions

Why would you eat *ice cream* while carrying a pair of *scissors* and walking through *the door* to cut a pair of *trousers* into pieces? Not because you are a wife after revenge, but to remember that the following nouns only have a plural form and any verb that follows will have to be in the third person plural:

lody	*ice cream*
nożyczki	*scissors*
drzwi	*door*
spodnie	*trousers*

For example:

Lody są pyszne.　　　*The ice cream is delicious.*
Nożyczki są ostre.　　*The scissors are sharp.*
Drzwi są otwarte.　　 *The door is open.* (Can also mean
　　　　　　　　　　　　The doors are open.)
Spodnie są za krótkie.　*The trousers are too short.*

Numerals – the '2–4 and 5+' rule

This may sound cryptic, but in fact it's a simple way to remember how Polish numerals and plurals work.

In Unit 11, you learned how Polish feminine nouns create their plural forms:

sypialnia (*bedroom*) – sypialnie
kuchnia (*kitchen*) – kuchnie
łazienka (*bathroom*) – łazienki

Why then in the dialogues when Maria describes the house does she say: **sześć sypialni** and not **sześć sypialnie?**

In Polish when you talk about two, three or four things, you use the basic nominative plural forms, but when you talk about five or more (up to 21) things you use the genitive plural forms. This applies to all three genders: masculine, feminine and neuter. Let's have a look at some examples.

Masculine nouns nominative singular (1)	Masculine nouns nominative plural (2–4)	Masculine nouns genitive plural (5+)
ogród (*garden*)	ogrody	ogrodów
park (*park*)	parki	parków
bank (*bank*)	banki	banków
klucz (*key*)	klucze	kluczy
pokój (*room*)	pokoje	pokoi
dom (*house*)	domy	domów

Feminine nouns nominative singular (1)	Feminine nouns nominative plural (2–4)	Feminine nouns genitive plural (5+)
sypialnia (*bedroom*)	sypialnie	sypialni
kuchnia (*kitchen*)	kuchnie	kuchni
łazienka (*bathroom*)	łazienki	łazienek
kaplica (*chapel*)	kaplice	kaplic
biblioteka (*library*)	biblioteki	bibliotek

Neuter nouns nominative singular (1)	Neuter nouns nominative plural (2–4)	Neuter nouns genitive plural (5+)
okno (*window*)	okna	okien
piwo (*beer*)	piwa	piw
pióro (*pen*)	pióra	piór
nazwisko (*surname*)	nazwiska	nazwisk

From the examples above you can see that while forming basic nominative plurals is reasonably straightforward (just replace -o with -a) the genitive form looks strange and somewhat unpredictable. A good Polish dictionary will state the genitive plural form of nouns.

There are, however, some exceptions to the rule explained above:

dziecko	*child*	dzieci	*children*
imię	*first name*	imiona	*first names*

Pronunciation guide Jak to wymówić?

Spelling and pronunciation of Polish surnames and place names

Hopefully, by following the advice given in previous units you are now able to read any Polish surnames or placenames, because Polish pronunciation rules work so consistently.

Listen and repeat

Kotomierz	Jarocin	Rzeszów	Tarnów	Łowicz	Łódź
Szczebrzeszyn	Dąbrowa	Żdżary	Karpacz	Bąkowiec	Chorzów
Wrocław	Szczecin	Łeba	Kołobrzeg	Gdańsk	Sandomierz
Międzyrzecz	Wałbrzych	Elbląg	Świnoujście	Kętrzyn	Gniezno

Listen and repeat

Zdzisław Mrożewski   Bożena Kleszczyńska
Andrzej Łapicki   Lech Wałęsa
Tadeusz Kotlarczyk   Przemysław Gliszcz
Małgorzata Gnuś   Jan Leszczyński
Jerzy Klimaszewski   Wojciech Trzebniewski
Adam Mickiewicz   Jerzy Krześniak
Juliusz Słowacki   Stanisław Grzegorzewski
Jadwiga Stępień   Mieczysław Tchórzewski
Józef Konarzewski   Katarzyna Wójcik
Teodor Korzeniowski   Grażyna Strzembosz
Grzegorz Siemianowski   Grzegorz Brzęczyszczykiewicz

Test yourself

Exercise 1

Translate the following plurals into Polish.

a *two gardens*: dwa _____
b *seven gardens*: siedem _____
c *three keys*: trzy _____
d *nine keys*: dziewięć _____

Exercise 2

Translate the following plurals into Polish.

a *two bathrooms*: dwie _____
b *six bathrooms*: sześć _____
c *four chapels*: cztery _____
d *ten chapels*: dziesięć _____

Exercise 3

Translate the following into Polish.

a *two windows*: dwa _____
b *seven windows*: siedem _____
c *four pens*: cztery _____
d *eight pens*: osiem _____

Exercise 4

Translate the following sentences into Polish. (blue cards)

a What a beautiful view!
b It was a beautiful house once.
c The house has a sitting room, a dining room and a bedroom.
d Is there a bathroom in the house?
e It looks like the house had a garden as well.
f The garden was behind the house.
g A small chapel stood in the park.
h What a pity the house is ruined.
i Have you got the key?
j Let's go inside.
k The door is open.

Exercise 5

Respond in Polish to the following English prompts. As before, you can check your answers and pronunciation on the recording. (yellow cards)

a Jaki piękny widok! (*Yes, it's very beautiful.*)
b Ile dwór miał sypialni? (*It had six bedrooms.*)
c Czy była łazienka w domu? (*Yes, there was a bathroom.*)
d Co jeszcze było w domu? (*A chapel, a library, a garden and a park.*)
e Gdzie był ogród? (*The garden was behind the house.*)
f Chodźmy do środka. (*Have you got the key?*)
g Czy chciałby pan mieszkać w kamienicy? (*No, I would like to live in a palace.*)

Exercise 6

Complete the following sentences. (green cards)

a Czy ma pan _____ (*key*)?
b Nie, ale _____ (*door*) są otwarte.
c We dworze było sześć _____ (*bedrooms*).
d Jaki piękny _____ (*view*)!
e Gdzie jest _____ (*bathroom*)?
f Czy jest _____ (*kitchen*) na parterze?
g Na prawo od domu były _____ (*stables*).
h _____ (*chapel*) stała w parku.

Did you know? (purple cards)

Polish vodka is probably the best in the world and the choice is bewildering: clear vodkas, sweet honey (Krupnik), nut (Orzechówka), cherry (Wiśniówka) and coffee (Rosolis) liqueurs, smooth herb flavoured bison grass vodka (Żubrówka) and Gold Wasser (Goldwasser), a sweet liqueur with flakes of gold floating in the bottle, to name just a few.

15

Wygram milion na loterii
I'll win a million on the lottery

In this unit you will learn
- *how to talk about the future*
- *how to express surprise*

In this unit you will learn how to express what will happen in the future.

Dialogue 1 **Dialog pierwszy**

Maria and Andrew go into the hallway of the manor house. They move slowly among the broken furniture and piles of rubble from the crumbling walls and the ceiling. They walk into the sitting room. The floor is littered with pieces of newspaper. Andrew picks up a page with a horoscope on it.

Vocabulary **Słówka**

Form in the dialogue	Dictionary form	English translation
wierzyć w + acc.	wierzyć > uwierzyć	*believe in*
horoskopy	horoskop	*horoscopes*
pomyślne	pomyślny	*favourable, positive*
znak [Zodiaku]	znak, Zodiak	*sign (of the Zodiac)*
byk		*bull, Taurus*
też		*too, also, as well*
Co ty powiesz!	co, ty, powiedzieć	*Fancy that!*

Andrew	Czy wierzysz w horoskopy?	*Do you believe in horoscopes?*
Maria	Nie, a ty?	*No. What about you?*
Andrew	Wierzę w horoskopy tylko kiedy są pomyślne. Jaki jest twój znak?	*I believe in horoscopes only when they are favourable. What's your sign?*
Maria	Byk.	*Taurus.*
Andrew	Co ty powiesz! Byk to też mój znak.	*Fancy that! Taurus is my sign, too.*

Dialogue 2 Dialog drugi

Andrew looks at the paper and starts reading.

Vocabulary Słówka

Form in the dialogue	Dictionary form	English translation
planeta		*planet*
weszła	wchodzić > wejść, w	*has moved into*
w + accusative		*into, to*
w sferę	w, sfera	*into the area, sphere, region*
podróży	podróż	*of travel, of journey(s)*
przyjaźni	przyjaźń	*of friendship*
odkryć	odkrycie	*of discoveries*
będziesz podróżować	być, podróżować > popodróżować	*you'll travel/be travelling*
w krainie	w, kraina	*in the land (poetic)*
uskrzydlonych rycerzy	uskrzydlony rycerz	*of winged knights*
znajdziesz	znajdować > znaleźć	*you'll find*
nowych przyjaciół	nowy przyjaciel	*new friends*
odkryjesz	odkrywać > odkryć	*you'll discover*
przeszłość		*the past*
odwiedzisz	odwiedzać > odwiedzić	*to visit*
stary dom		*an old house*

jeszcze		*still, besides, more, yet*
wygram	wygrywać > wygrać	*I'll win*
milion		*a million*
na loterii	loteria	*in a/the lottery*
co za		*what sort of, what*
nonsens		*rubbish, nonsense*
poza tym	poza, to	*besides (that)*
pewnie	pewny	*certainly, surely*
z dziesięć lat	rok/lato	*ten years or so*
więc		*so*
bez znaczenia	znaczenie	*meaningless, without significance*

Andrew	'Twoja planeta Wenus weszła w sferę podróży, przyjaźni i odkryć. Będziesz podróżować z kimś bliskim w krainie uskrzydlonych rycerzy. Znajdziesz nowych przyjaciół.	*'Your planet Venus has entered the sphere of travels, friendship and discoveries. You will be travelling with someone close to you in the land of winged knights. You'll find new friends.*
	Odkryjesz przeszłość. Odwiedzisz stary dom.' (sarkastycznie) I jeszcze wygram million na loterii … Co za nonsens!	*You'll discover the past. You'll visit an old house.' (mockingly) I'll also win a million in a lottery … What nonsense!*
Maria	A poza tym, ten horoskop ma pewnie z dziesięć lat, więc jest bez znaczenia.	*And apart from that, this horoscope is about ten years old so it's meaningless.*

Dialogue 3 **Dialog trzeci**

Suddenly, Maria and Andrew hear a noise. They look out of the window and see a car pulling into the drive. Both go back to the entrance hall. The door opens and Ewa walks in. Maria is completely amazed.

Vocabulary **Słówka**

Form in the dialogue	Dictionary form	English translation
fantastyczną wiadomość	fantastyczna wiadomość	a fantastic (piece) of news
właścicielem	właściciel	owner
wiary	wiara	belief, faith
Nie do wiary!		I can't believe it!
wszystko		everything, all

Maria	Co ty tu robisz?	*What are you doing here?*
Ewa	Mam dla was fantastyczną wiadomość!	*I've got a fantastic piece of news for you.*
Andrew	Jaką wiadomość?	*What sort of news?*
Ewa	Wiem, kto jest właścicielem tego dworu.	*I know who is the owner of the mansion.*
Maria	Nie do wiary!	*I can't believe it!*
Ewa	Ale to nie wszystko. Wiem też, kim jest pana krewna.	*But that's not all. I also know who your relative is.*

◉ CD2, TR 57

Dialogue 4 **Dialog czwarty**

Ewa pauses for a moment. Maria and Andrew look at her impatiently.

Vocabulary **Słówka**

Form in the dialogue	Dictionary form	English translation
no		*well, then, yes (colloquial)*
nie trzymaj nas	trzymać, my	*don't keep us*
w napięciu	napięcie; napinać > napiąć	*in suspense*
zaraz		*in a minute*
wszystko		*everything*
opowiem	opowiadać > opowiedzieć	*tell*

◆ CD2, TK 58

Maria	No, nie trzymaj nas w napięciu!	*Don't keep us in suspense!*
Ewa	Chwileczkę.	*Just a minute.*
	Zaraz wam wszystko opowiem.	*I'll tell you everything in a minute.*

Let's practise

▶ Copy the dialogues (both the Polish and English parts) onto small pieces of paper.

▶ Mix the pieces and reconstruct the dialogues correctly (both parts).

▶ Mix the pieces again and reconstruct the Polish side of the dialogues.

▶ Separate the Polish and English parts of the dialogues. Turn the Polish parts face down and mix them again. Turn them face up at random and translate into English.

▶ Do the same exercise with the English parts of the dialogues.

◄) CD2, TR 59

Listen and repeat

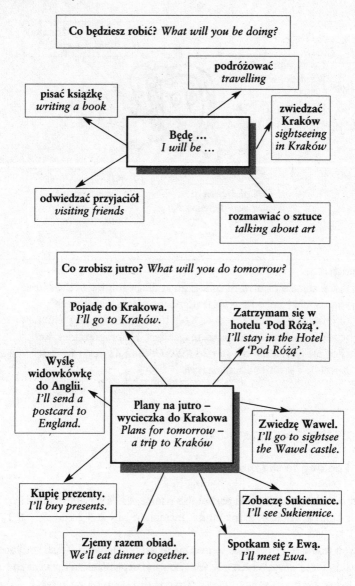

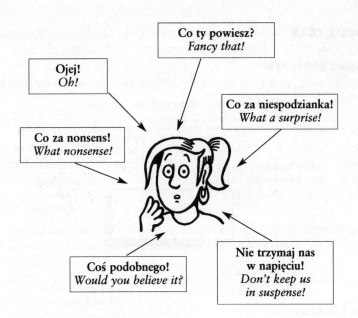

Insight

If you started your word collection at the beginning of the course you should have quite a large number of cards with a wealth of information on them by now. Keep the collection going with new words you learn from books, magazines, TV programmes, web sites, etc. If you haven't started the collection it's never too late. It will be a great revision exercise.

How the language works

Looking to the future

We have reached the final part of this course, so it's very fitting that in this unit we will look to the future (metaphorically and grammatically).

If you would like to express something in a future tense in Polish you can do it in three ways. Which way you choose is dependent on the verb and whether it is perfective or imperfective. As this is a complex subject, in this unit we will look at two of the ways of creating the future tense. However, if you would like to know the third way refer to the Grammar appendix.

To start with you need to know how the verb **być** is formed in the future tense:

ja	będę	*I will be*	my	będziemy	*we will be*
ty	będziesz	*you will be*	wy	będziecie	*you will be*
on	będzie	*he will be*	oni/one	będą	*they will be*
ona	będzie	*she will be*			
ono	będzie	*it will be*			

For imperfective verbs, you form the future tense with an appropriate form of **być** (*to be*) in the future tense + a verb in the infinitive form.

For example:

[ja] będę czekać	*I'll be waiting*
[ja] będę czytać	*I'll be reading*
Ewa będzie kupować	*Ewa will be buying*
one będą mieszkać	*they will be living*

The second way of creating the future tense is for perfective verbs. Before we explain the rule, let's have a look at some examples and compare the two verbs: imperfective **czekać** and perfective **zaczekać**.

◆) CD2, TR 60

Listen and repeat

Present tense czekać (imperfective)	Future tense zaczekać (perfective)
ja czekam (*I wait*)	ja zaczekam (*I will wait*)
ty czekasz (*you wait*)	ty zaczekasz (*you will wait*)
on czeka (*he waits*)	on zaczeka (*he will wait*)
ona czeka (*she waits*)	ona zaczeka (*she will wait*)
ono czeka (*it waits*)	ono zaczeka (*it will wait*)

Present tense czekać (imperfective)	Future tense zaczekać (perfective)
my czekamy (*we wait*)	my zaczekamy (*we will wait*)
wy czekacie (*you wait*)	wy zaczekacie (*you will wait*)
oni/one czekają (*they wait*)	oni/one zaczekają (*they will wait*)

To create the future tense for perfective verbs you add a present tense ending to a perfective verb. Although it looks like a present tense, it will not have a present tense meaning. (From Unit 13 we know that perfective verbs don't have a present tense.)

Let's look at some more examples (for simplicity the following examples are all for the first person singular – *I*):

Present tense	Imperfective	Future tense	Perfective
gotować	*to cook*	ugotować	
Gotuję obiad.	*I'm cooking dinner.*	Ugotuję obiad.	*I will cook dinner.*
jeść	*to eat*	zjeść	
Jem obiad.	*I'm eating dinner.*	Zjem obiad.	*I will eat dinner.*
czytać	*to read*	przeczytać	
Czytam książkę.	*I'm reading a book.*	Przeczytam książkę.	*I will read a book.*
budować	*to build*	zbudować	
Buduję dom.	*I'm building a house.*	Zbuduję dom.	*I will build a house.*

The third way of creating a future tense in Polish is for imperfective verbs (it's different from the method above) and it can be described as 'back to the future'. If you would like to know more, please refer to the Grammar Appendix where it is explained in detail.

Pronunciation guide **Jak to wymówić?**

Polish tongue twisters

Hopefully, you will have plenty of opportunity to revise and practise Polish pronunciation in the future. If you have Polish friends or relatives, you may already know that Poles sometimes like asking their English-speaking friends to say one of the numerous Polish tongue twisters. Usually, this results in a moment of cheap entertainment at your expense. But no longer. Are you ready?

W Szczebrzeszynie, chrząszcz brzmi w trzcinie.
(In Szczebrzeszyn a beetle is buzzing in the reed.)

Król Karol kupił królowej Karolinie korale koloru koralowego.
(King Charles bought Queen Caroline a necklace in the colour of coral.)

Dzięcioł pień ciął.
(A woodpecker was cutting a tree trunk.)

Jerzy nie wierzy, że na wieży leży gniazdo jeży.
(George doesn't believe that on the (top of) the tower lies a nest of hedgehogs.)

Drewniana skrzynia była skrzętnie schowana pod skrzypiącymi schodami.
(A wooden crate was carefully hidden under creaking stairs.)

Test yourself

Exercise 1

Translate the following sentences into Polish. (blue cards)

a Do you believe in horoscopes?
b Yes, I believe in horoscopes.
c No, I don't (believe).
d What's your sign (of the Zodiac)?
e You will be travelling to Kraków with a friend.
f You will find new friends.
g I will win a million on the lottery.
h I would like to win a million on the lottery.
i What nonsense!
j What a surprise!
k Fancy that!
l I don't understand.
m What are you doing here?

◆) CD2, TR 62

Exercise 2

Respond in Polish to the following English prompts. Check your answers and pronunciation on the recording. (yellow cards)

a Czy wierzysz w horoskopy?
(*No I don't.*)
b Jaki jest twój znak?
(*Taurus.*)
c Czy chciałbyś wygrać milion na loterii?
(*Yes, I would like.*)
d Byk to też mój znak.
(*Fancy that!*)
e Co mówi twój horoskop?
(*It says I will be travelling and I will find new friends.*)
f Wiem, kto jest właścicielem dworu.
(*I can't believe it.*)

Exercise 3

Complete the following sentences. (green cards)

a Jaki jest twój _____?
b Wygrasz milion na _____.
c Wierzę w horoskopy, kiedy są _____.
d Nie trzymaj nas w _____!
e Mam dla was fantastyczną _____.
f Wiem, kto jest _____ tego dworu.
g Co za kompletny _____!

Well, this is the last unit of the course and the end of the story so far. However, there are still some unanswered questions: Who do you think Andrew's cousin is? Is it Maria, or Ewa or perhaps someone completely different? What's going to happen to the house? Is Andrew going to be its owner?

Put all you have learned in this course into practice and try to write the ending to this story. Good luck with your creative work!

Did you know? (purple cards)

▶ Poland is a country of rich heritage in terms of history, culture and natural habitat.
▶ Poland has 23 National Parks.
▶ Part of the last primeval forest in Europe (Białowieża) is in Poland.
▶ Poland has a desert (Pustynia Błędowska) and a Jurassic Trail.
▶ Poland also possesses a unique and amazing landscape of rolling white dunes that are visible even from outer space.
▶ Poland is the place to visit if you would like to see wolves, brown bears, lynx, elk, white and black storks, all in their natural habitats.
▶ Poland is the only place in the world where you can find banded (striped) flint also called 'Polish diamond'. Mined 3,000 years ago as a natural material for making tools, it has recently been made fashionable by the likes of Victoria Beckham and Robbie Williams who wear it as jewellery.

Grammar appendix

For many students, grammar is a bit like a latest gadget manual – an attempt to make the user understand all the wonderful features the newly purchased machine offers, but generally regarded as difficult to understand and rather dull.

You can get by in a foreign language simply by using a limited number of words and phrases learned by heart from a phrase book, however without some knowledge of how the language works you will not be able to generate your own sentences. It's a bit like visiting a beautiful stately home and just staying in the hallway – the rest of house remains beyond your reach because you don't know how to open the door.

Hopefully, this Grammar appendix will prove to be a good guide in your journey through Polish. It is meant to be an additional reference tool. Hopefully it will make the experience of learning Polish more rewarding.

Throughout the course you will come across a number of terms you may or may not be familiar with: nouns, verbs, perfective and imperfective types, adjectives, adverbs, etc. This section of the book is intended to organize the information in a way that is easy to find and understand.

Definite and indefinite articles ('a', 'an', 'the')

Polish doesn't have definite or indefinite articles. It's the context that allows you to interpret whether a noun is definite or indefinite. **Kobieta** can be *a woman* as well as *the woman*.

Nouns

A noun is a word, which names or refers to:

▶ a person (**Anglik** *an Englishman*, **detektyw** *a detective*, **mężczyzna** *a man*, **kobieta** *a woman*, **dziecko** *a child*)

- an object (**stół** *a table*, **książka** *a book*, **samochód** *a car*)
- an animal or a plant (**pies** *a dog*, **kot** *a cat*, **tulipan** *a tulip*)
- an abstract concept (**chwila** *a moment*)
- a place (**Anglia** *England*, **Polska** *Poland*)
- a natural phenomenon (**mgła** *fog*), etc.

There are two important things to know about nouns:

1 They have a gender regardless of whether they are animate or inanimate (person or non-person). There are three genders: masculine, feminine and neuter. For example, the following nouns are masculine:

detektyw	*a detective*
stół	*a table*
pies	*a dog*
dom	*a house*
samochód	*a car*

Typically, masculine nouns end in a consonant (e.g. **-b, -k, -l, -w, -m**) but there are some exceptions such as **dentysta** (*a dentist*), **kierowca** (*a driver*) and **mężczyzna** (*a man*).

The following nouns are feminine:

kobieta	*a woman*
emerytka	*a retired female*
książka	*a book*
córka	*a daughter*
ulica	*a street*

Most feminine nouns end in **-a**.

The following nouns are neuter:

nazwisko	*surname*
piwo	*beer/lager*
wino	*wine*
mleko	*milk*
dziecko	*child*

Typically, neuter nouns end in -o or -e.

2 Nouns have different forms for expressing grammatical cases (seven in total) related to the function they play in the sentence. This is a vast and complex subject, which tends to be rather difficult and confusing for many English native speakers.

The following guide is not exhaustive but it is intended to give you a helping hand on the subject of cases.

Nominative (who?/what?) **Mianownik (kto?/co?)**
Generally, the nominative plays the role of a subject in a sentence.

To jest **detektyw**.   *This is a detective.*

Genitive (of who?/of what?) **Dopełniacz (kogo?/czego?)**
The genitive case is used:

▶ to express possession (when English uses *'s* or *of*)
▶ to express the absence or lack of something

For example:

Nie ma **czasu**.   *There's no time.*
Nie mam **pieniędzy**.   *I haven't got any money.*

▶ with expressions of quantity

For example:

szklanka **wody**   *a glass of water*
kilo **bananów**   *a kilo of bananas*
dużo **ludzi**   *lots of people*

▶ after the number five and upwards

For example:

pięć **domów**   *five houses*

▶ with some prepositions

od	from	daleko od **domu**	far from home
do	to	do **domu**	(to) home
dla	for	dla **mamy**	for Mum
naprzeciw (ko)	opposite	naprzeciwko **domu**	opposite the house
obok	next to	obok **domu**	next to the house
blisko	near	blisko **domu**	near the house
niedaleko	not far from	niedaleko **domu**	not far from the house
u	at	u **przyjaciół**	at friends'
wokół	around	wokół **domu**	around the house
z/ze	from	z **Londynu**	from London

Dative (to whom?/to what?) **Celownik (komu?/czemu?)**
The dative is used:

▶ to express an indirect object

For example:

Andrew daje **Marii** wizytówkę.   *Andrew gives his business card to Maria.*

▶ in certain impersonal expressions

For example:

Jest **mi** słabo.	*I feel faint.*
Bardzo **mi** miło.	*Pleased to meet you.*
Było **mu** duszno.	*He needed some air.*
Nudzi **mi** się.	*I'm bored.*
Wszystkim jest trudno.	*We all find it difficult.*

Accusative (whom?/what?) **Biernik (kogo?/co?)**
The accusative is used to express the direct object. It is used:

▶ after **mieć** (*to have*)

For example:

Mam **samochód**.	*I've got a car.*
Mam **brata**.	*I've got a brother.*

▶ with prepositions related to verbs of motion

Idę na **spacer**.	*I'm going for a walk.*

▶ with days of the week

w **sobotę**	*on Saturday*
we **wtorek**	*on Tuesday*

▶ when referring to playing games

grać w **tenisa**	*play tennis*

(This list doesn't exhaust all the possibilities but it's a good start.)

Instrumental ((with) whom?/(with) what?) **Narzędnik ((z) kim?/(z) czym?)**
The instrumental case is used:

▶ after **być** (*to be*) to express nationality, profession or identity

For example:

Jestem **Anglikiem**.	*I'm English.*
Jestem **detektywem**.	*I'm a detective.*
Azor jest **dobrym psem**.	*Azor is a good dog.*

▶ with expressions of time

For example:

wieczorem	*in the evening*
wiosną	*in the spring*
nocą	*at night*

▶ to express means by which an action is performed

For example:

Jadę **autobusem**.	*I'm going by bus.*
Płacę **kartą kredytową**.	*I'm paying with a credit card*

Locative (about whom?/about what?/where?) **Miejscownik (o kim?/o czym?/gdzie?)**
The locative is used:

▶ to indicate the time and the place of the action after the following prepositions:

na	na **przytanku**	*at the bus stop*
	na **dworcu**	*at the railway station*
po	po **obiedzie**	*after dinner*
	po **południu**	*in the afternoon*
przy	przy **hotelu**	*by the hotel*
	przy **fotelu**	*by the armchair*
w	w **styczniu**	*in January*
	w 2008 **roku**	*in 2008*

Nouns in the locative case are always preceded by a preposition.

Vocative **Wołacz** – *the attention-getting case*
The vocative is used to address whoever we are speaking or writing to directly:

Basiu! Kasiu! Mario! Panie Andrzeju! Ewo!

Droga **Barbaro!**	*Dear Barbara!*
Kochana **Mamusiu!**	*Beloved Mum!*
Szanowni **Państwo!**	*Dear ladies and gentlemen!*
Ty **idioto!**	*You idiot!*
Ty **świnio!**	*You swine!*

Giving nouns appropriate endings is called declension (or declination) and here are three examples of nouns you have met in the course.

Masculine nouns

Case	Singular	Plural
Nominative	detektyw	detektywi
Genitive	detektywa	detektywów
Dative	detektywowi	detektywom
Accusative	detektywa	detektywów
Instrumental	detektywem	detektywami
Locative	detektywie	detektywach
Vocative	detektywie!	detektywi!

Feminine nouns

Case	Singular	Plural
Nominative	studentka	studentki
Genitive	studentki	studentek
Dative	studentce	studentkom
Accusative	studentkę	studentki
Instrumental	studentką	studentkami
Locative	studentce	studentkach
Vocative	studentko!	studentki!

Neuter nouns

Case	Singular	Plural
Nominative	nazwisko	nazwiska
Genitive	nazwiska	nazwisk
Dative	nazwisku	nazwiskom
Accusative	nazwisko	nazwiska
Instrumental	nazwiskiem	nazwiskami
Locative	nazwisku	nazwiskach
Vocative	nazwisko!	nazwiska!

Adjectives

Adjectives are natural companions to nouns as they help describe nouns:

angielski detektyw	*English detective*
interesująca wiadomość	*interesting news*
zimne piwo	*cold beer*

Just like nouns, adjectives have three genders and they usually agree with the gender of the noun:

angielski detektyw (masculine)	*English detective*
angielska książka (feminine)	*English book*
angielskie piwo (neuter)	*English beer*

In most cases adjectives precede nouns (<u>**nowy**</u> samochód – *a <u>new</u> car*) but in some cases, usually when a noun means several things and the adjective clarifies the meaning, the adjective will follow the noun. For example, **straż** can mean a *fire service*, or *municipal guard* and the adjective will clarify the meaning:

straż pożarna	*fire service*
Straż miejska	*municipal guard*

Pronouns

Pronouns refer to things without naming them. Whereas **detektyw** (detective) is a noun, **on** (*he*) is a pronoun. There are many different categories of pronouns, such as personal pronouns (**ja** (*I*), **oni** and **one** (*they*)) and possessive pronouns (**mój** (*my*), **twój** (*your*)).

Personal pronoun	Possessive pronoun – masculine	Possessive pronoun – feminine	Possessive pronoun – neuter
ja (*I*)	mój (*my*)	moja	moje
ty (*you*)	twój (*your*)	twoja	twoje
on (*he*)	jego (*his*)	n/a	n/a
ona (*she*)	n/a	jej (her)	n/a
ono (*it*)	n/a	n/a	jego (its)
my (*we*)	nasz (*our*)	nasza	nasze
wy (*you*)	wasz (*your*)	wasza	wasze
oni/one (*they*)	ich (*their*)	ich	ich

Declination of masculine possessive pronoun, adjective and noun:

Nominative	mój	angielski	detektyw
Genitive	mojego	angielskiego	detektywa
Dative	mojemu	angielskiemu	detektywowi
Accusative	mojego	angielskiego	detektywa
Instrumental	moim	angielskim	detektywem
Locative	moim	angielskim	detektywie
Vocative	O mój	angielski	detektywie!

Declination of feminine possessive pronoun, adjective and noun:

Nominative	moja	angielska	książka
Genitive	mojej	angielskiej	książki
Dative	mojej	angielskiej	książce
Accusative	moją	angielską	książkę
Instrumental	moją	angielską	książką
Locative	mojej	angielskiej	książce
Vocative	O moja	angielska	książko!

Nominative	moje	angielskie	piwo
Genitive	mojego	angielskiego	piwa
Dative	mojemu	angielskiemu	piwu
Accusative	moje	angielskie	piwo
Instrumental	moim	angielskim	piwem
Locative	moim	angielskim	piwie
Vocative	O moje	angielskie	piwo!

Verbs

Verbs are words that refer to action (*to go, to sit, to write, to speak, to love, to hate*, etc). Verbs have forms for different tenses (past, present or future).

For example:

pojechać	*to go*
pojechałem	*I went*
pojadę	*I will go*

Verbs have different forms for different 'persons' (*I, you, he, she*, etc.):

ja jadę	*I go*	my jedziemy	*we go*
ty jedziesz	*you* (singular) *go*	wy jedziecie	*you* (plural) *go*
on jedzie	*he goes*	oni/one jadą	*they go*
ona jedzie	*she goes*		
ono jedzie	*it goes*		

There are also other forms, such as the infinitive (dictionary) form:

czytać	*to read*
pisać	*to write*
jeść	*to eat*

'Aspect' is a matter of how a verb presents an action or situation: not summed up (imperfective) or summed up (perfective). Imperfective verbs have a present tense, as well as a future and a past. Perfective verbs in Polish have no present tense for referring to present time but have a simple future.

For example:

Czytam książkę	*I'm reading a book. (present)*
Czytałem książkę.	*I was reading a book. (past)*
Będę cztać książkę.	*I will be reading a book. (future)*
Przeczytałem książkę.	*I read a book. (past)*
Przeczytam książkę.	*I will read a book. (future)*

Reflexive verbs describe the action happening to ourselves or to a group of specific people. You can easily recognize a reflexive verb because of the presence of **się**. Bear in mind that not all verbs that are reflexive in Polish are automatically reflexive in English:

obawiam się	*I'm afraid*
myję się	*I'm washing myself*
pakuję się	*I'm packing*
spotkamy się	*we will meet*

Się is never stressed and tends to blend with the verb that precedes it.

Adverbs

Just as adjectives are closely associated with nouns, adverbs are natural companions to verbs. What's more, adverbs are often derived from adjectives:

Adjective	**Adverb**
zimne piwo *(cold beer)*	Jest zimno. *(It's cold.)*
piękna pogoda *(lovely weather)*	Jest pięknie. *(It's lovely.)*
prosta droga *(straight road)*	iść prosto *(to go straight ahead)*
krótkie włosy *(short hair)*	przyjechać na krótko *(to come for a short period of time)*
daleki kuzyn *(a distant relative)*	daleko stąd *(far away from here)*

Adverbials

Adverbials are words or phrases that provide additional information by answering questions such as:

Kiedy?	**When?**
dzisiaj	today
wczoraj	yesterday
jutro	tomorrow
zaraz	in a moment
często	often
w piątek	on Friday

Gdzie?	**Where?**
daleko	far away
niedaleko	not far
blisko	near
tutaj	here
tam	over there
na Rynku	in the Market Square
w Polsce	in Poland

Jak?	**How?**
wolno	slowly
szybko	quickly
spokojnie	calmly
prosto	straight ahead
Dlaczego?	Why?
żeby odpoczął	so he could rest

Ile?	**How much/many?**
dużo	a lot
mało	a little

Please note that not all adverbials are adverbs.

For example:

w piątek	*on Friday*
w Polsce	*in Poland*
na Rynku	*in the Market Square*

Numbers

Numbers in Polish represent one of the more complex subjects. They align themselves to nouns, matching their gender. There are also two main types of numbers (cardinal numbers which tell 'how many' and show quantity – one, two, three, etc. and ordinal numbers which tell the order of things – first, second, third, etc.) to deal with. Treat the following table as a starting point.

Number	Cardinal	Ordinal (-st, -nd, -rd, -th) *in masculine form*
1	jeden (*one*)	pierwszy (*first*)
2	dwa	drugi
3	trzy	trzeci
4	cztery	czwarty
5	pięć	piąty
6	sześć	szósty
7	siedem	siódmy
8	osiem	ósmy
9	dziewięć	dziewiąty
10	dziesięć	dziesiąty
11	jedenaście	jedenasty
12	dwanaście	dwunasty
13	trzynaście	trzynasty
14	czternaście	czternasty
15	piętnaście	piętnasty
16	szesnaście	szesnasty
17	siedemnaście	siedemnasty
18	osiemnaście	osiemnasty

Number	Cardinal	Ordinal (-st, -nd, -rd, -th) in masculine form
19	dziewiętnaście	dziewiętnasty
20	dwadzieścia	dwudziesty
30	trzydzieści	trzydziesty
40	czterdzieści	czterdziesty
50	pięćdziesiąt	pięćdziesiąty
60	sześćdziesiąt	sześćdziesiąty
70	siedemdziesiąt	siedemdziesiąty
80	osiemdziesiąt	osiemdziesiąty
90	dziewięćdziesiąt	dziewięćdziesiąty
100	sto	setny
23	dwadzieścia trzy	dwudziesty trzeci
45	czterdzieści pięć	czterdziesty piąty
78	siedemdziesiąt osiem	siedemdziesiąty ósmy
91	dziewięćdziesiąt jeden	dziewięćdziesiąty pierwszy

Back to the future – a future tense

In Unit 15 you were introduced to the future tense in Polish and you already know that there are three ways of creating it in Polish: one way for *perfective* verbs and two ways for *imperfective* verbs. 'Back to the future' is a very fitting title because one way of describing the future is to combine the future tense of **być** with a verb in its past tense.

This is how **być** is formed for all persons in the future tense:

być – future form

ja	będę	*I will be*	my	będziemy	*we will be*
ty	będziesz	*you will be*	wy	będziecie	*you will be*
on	będzie	*he will be*	oni/one	będą	*they will be*
ona	będzie	*she will be*			
ono	będzie	*it will be*			

For imperfective verbs you need an appropriate form of the future tense of **być** + infinitive:

będę czekać	*I'll be waiting*
będę czytać	*I'll be reading*
Ewa będzie kupować	*Ewa will be buying*
one będą mieszkać	*they will be living*

Verb infinitive	Verb third person sing./ plural masculine/ feminine/neuter	Example	
czekać (*to wait*)	czekał/czekała/ czekało czekali/czekały	*I, you, etc. will be waiting*	*for the bus.*
		Ja będę czekał/ czekała	
		Ty będziesz czekał/ czekała	
		On będzie czekał	
		Ona będzie czekała	na
		Ono będzie czekało	autobus.
		My będziemy czekali	
		Wy będziecie czekali	
		Oni będą czekali	
		One będą czekały	

Alternatively, you can use the future tense of **być** + verb in the third person (singular or plural) of the past tense:

To create the future tense for perfective verbs you add a present tense ending to a perfective verb. Although it looks like a present tense, it will not have a present tense meaning. (From Unit 13 we know that perfective verbs don't have a present tense.)

For simplicity the following examples are all for the first person singular – *I*:

Present tense		Future tense	
Gotuję obiad	*I'm cooking dinner.*	Ugotuję obiad.	*I will cook dinner.*
Jem obiad	*I'm eating dinner.*	Zjem obiad	*I will eat dinner.*
Czytam książkę.	*I'm reading a book.*	Przeczytam książkę.	*I will read a book.*
Buduję dom.	*I'm building a house.*	Zbuduję dom.	*I will build a house.*

Examples of simple sentence patterns in Polish

To + *być* ('to be') + noun (nominative)
To + jest + detektyw. (nominative)
This + is + a detective.

To + są + słynne obrazy. (adjective + noun nom.)
These + are + famous paintings.

Subject + *być* ('to be') + noun (instrumental)
Andrew (subject) + jest + detektywem. (noun in the instrumental form)
Andrew + is + a detective.

Maria (subject) + jest + Polką. (noun instrumental)
Maria + is + Polish.

Tom (subject) + jest + Anglikiem. (noun instrumental)
Tom + is + English.

Tom (subject) + jest + studentem. (noun instrumental)
Tom + is + a student.

Subject + *mieć* ('to have') + noun (accusative)
Ja (subject) + mam + dokument. (noun accusative)
I + have + a document.

Maria (subject) + ma + rodzinę. (noun accusative)
Maria + has + a family.

Andrew (subject) + ma + rodzinne dokumenty. (adjective + noun accusative)
Andrew + has + family documents.

Subject + *nie mieć* **('to have not') + noun (genitive)**
Ja (subject) + nie mam + dokumentu. (genitive)
I + haven't got + a document.

Andrew (subject) + nie ma + czasu. (genitive)
Andrew + hasn't got + time.

Maria (subject) + nie ma + rodziny. (genitive)
Maria + hasn't got + a family.

Poproszę **+ noun (accusative)**
Poproszę + sok. (noun accusative)
Can I have + juice?

Poproszę + mapę. (noun accusative)
Can I have + a map?

Subject + *musieć* **('must') + verb (infinitive) + rest of the sentence (RS)**
If the rest of the sentence is a noun, it will be in the accusative.

Maria (subject) + musi + zwiedzić (verb – infinitive) + Kraków. (RS/acc)
Maria + must + visit + Kraków.

Andrew (subject) + musi + wymienić (verb – infinitive) + pieniądze. (RS/acc)
Andrew + must + exchange + money.

Subject + *nie musieć* **('do not have to') + verb (infinitive) + RS**
If RS is a noun then it will be in the genitive.

Maria (subject) + nie musi + zwiedzić (verb – infinitive) + Krakowa.
Maria + doesn't have to + visit + Kraków.

Andrew (subject) + nie musi + wymienić (verb – infinitive) + pieniędzy.
Andrew + doesn't have to + exchange + money.

Note: **Chciał(a)by** follows the same pattern as **musieć** (above).

Subject + *lubić* **('to like') + noun (accusative)**
Maria (subject) + lubi + czekoladę. (noun acc.)
Maria + likes + chocolate.

Andrew (subject) + lubi + sernik. (noun acc.)
Andrew + likes + cheesecake.

Subject + *nie lubić* **('do not like') + noun (genitive)**
Maria (subject) + nie lubi + czekolady. (noun gen.)
Maria + doesn't like + chocolate.

Andrew (subject) + nie lubi + sernika. (noun gen.)
Andrew + doesn't like + cheesecake.

Subject + *lubić* **('to like') + verb (infinitive/imperfective) + RS**
Maria (subject) + lubi + czytać (verb) + książki. (RS/Acc.)
Maria + likes + reading + books.

Andrew (subject) + lubi + zwiedzać (verb) + Kraków. (RS/Acc.)
Andrew + likes + visiting + Kraków.

Subject + *nie lubić* **('do not like') + verb (infinitive/
imperfective) + RS**
Maria (subject) + nie lubi + czytać (verb inf./imperf.) + książek. (RS/gen.)
Maria + doesn't like + reading + books.

Andrew (subject) + nie lubi + zwiedzać (verb) + Krakowa. (RS/gen.)
Andrew + doesn't like + visiting + Kraków.

Time

In Polish, time is described by using ordinal numbers ending in -a.
Godzina (*hour*) is grammatically feminine so the number aligns itself
with a feminine ending:

Która godzina?	*What time is it now?*
1:00	pierwsza
2:00	druga
3:00	trzecia
4:00	czwarta
5:00	piąta
6:00	szósta
7:00	siódma
8:00	ósma
9:00	dziewiąta
10:00	dziesiąta
11:00	jedenasta
12:00	dwunasta

If you want to ask at what time something happens you need to use:

O której godzinie? *At what time?*

The -**ej** ending is a clue to how the ending will change from -**a** to -**ej**.
See the examples:

at 1:00	o pierwszej
at 2:00	o drugiej
at 3:00	o trzeciej
at 4:00	o czwartej
at 5:00	o piątej
at 6:00	o szóstej
at 7:00	o siódmej
at 8:00	o ósmej
at 9:00	o dziewiątej
at 10:00	o dziesiątej
at 11:00	o jedenastej
at 12:00	o dwunastej

'2–4 and 5+' rule

In Polish when you talk about two, three or four things, you use basic nominative plural forms, but when you talk about five or more (up to 21) things you use the genitive plural forms. The numbers 22, 23 and 24 follow the same pattern as two, three and four, and so on.

2	dwa obrazy	*two paintings*
3	trzy obrazy	
4	cztery obrazy	
5–21	pięć obrazów–dwadzieścia jeden obrazów	
22	dwadzieścia dwa obrazy	
23	dwadzieścia trzy obrazy	
24	dwadzieścia cztery obrazy	

Test yourself revision exercises

Exercise 1

Put each first name with the matching surname.

a	Danuta	Kosiński/Kosińska
b	Tomasz	Dąbrowski/Dąbrowska
c	Andrzej	Kosiarski/Kosiarska
d	Ewa	Kowalski/Kowalska
e	Krzysztof	Jakubowski/Jakubowska
f	Edward	Paderewski/Paderewska
g	Maria	Słomczyński/Słomczyńska
h	Barbara	Jaworski/Jaworska

Exercise 2

Translate the following into English.

a Jestem Janusz Kowalczyk.
b Bardzo mi miło.
c Nie jestem Polakiem. Jestem Anglikiem.
d Mam polskie korzenie.
e Andrzej jest emerytem.
f Maria jest Polką.
g Czym się pan zajmuje?

Exercise 3

Which of the following could be said by a man, and which by a woman?

a Jestem zmęczony.
b Jestem zmęczona.
c Jestem emerytem.

d Jestem emerytką.
e Jestem Walijczykiem.
f Jestem Irlandką.

Exercise 4

Translate the following into English, taking care over which begins with *he* and which with *she*.

a Jestem lekarzem.
b Jest głodny.
c Jest pracowita.
d Jest Szkotką.
e Jest zajęta.
f Jest studentką.
g Jest aktorem.
h Jest lekarzem.

Exercise 5

Put the appropriate word or phrase from the left-hand column into the sentence on the right.

a mój pies/moim psem   To jest _____.
b mój kot/moim kotem   To jest _____.
c moja rodzina/moją rodziną   To jest _____.
d jest/to jest   _____ moja córka.
e medycyna/medycynę   Studiuje _____.
f studentem/studentką   Maria jest _____.
g to/ten Mariah   _____ moja siostra.
h ładny/ładna   Grażyna jest _____.
i ładna dziewczyna/ładną dziewczyną   Zosia jest _____.
j przystojny/przystojnym   Janusz jest _____.
k to/ten   Janusz _____ przystojny mężczyzna.

Exercise 6

Select the appropriate form from the left-hand column to fill the gap(s) in the sentence on the right.

a	rodzina/rodzinę	Maria ma w Polsce _____.
b	rodzina/rodziny	Pan nie ma w Polsce _____?
c	jaki/jaka/jakie	_____ to problem?
d	jaki/jaka/jakie	_____ kot?
e	żaden/żadna/żadne	_____ fotografia?
f	jakieś/jakichś	Czy ma pan przy sobie (*with/on you*) _____ dokumenty?
g	dokument/dokumenty fotografia/fotografie	To są _____ i _____.
h	na/w/do	Państwo są _____ emeryturze?
i	adres/adresu	Przepraszam, nie mam _____.
j	adres/adresu	Proszę, to jest _____.
k	na/w/do	Pani ma _____ imię Agnieszka?
l	rencista/rencistką	Moja mama jest _____.
m	rencistka/rencista	Mój ojciec to _____.
n	samochód/samochodu	Nie mamy _____.

Exercise 7

Translate the following into English.

- **a** Umiem.
- **b** Rozumieją.
- **c** Nie rozumiemy.
- **d** Umiecie?
- **e** Mam!
- **f** Masz!
- **g** Jak pani ma na imię?
- **h** Mam dobrą pracę.
- **i** Mają dokumenty.

Exercise 8

Translate the following into English.

a Co pan musi zrobić?
b Muszę wrócić do domu.
c Musimy się spotkać.
d Musimy.
e Muszę wymienić pieniądze.
f Nie, nie musi pan.
g Chcę się rozpakować.
h Koniecznie?

Exercise 9

Choose the appropriate word from the left-hand column to complete the sentence on the right.

a musi/musicie   Dlaczego _____ pani iść?
b muszę/muszą   Oni _____ już iść.
c musisz/muszą   (Ty) nie _____ się od razu (*immediately*) rozpakować.
d muszę/musimy   A my _____ koniecznie zadzwonić do domu.
e pan/panowie   Czy _____ musi już iść.
f spotkać/zwiedzić   Musimy się _____ znowu.
g spotkać/zwiedzić   Muszą państwo _____ Wrocław.

Exercise 10

Przepraszam (*Sorry*) literally means *I apologize*. Say the following in Polish.

a He apologizes.
b They're apologizing.
c We're apologizing.
d Why doesn't she apologize?

Exercise 11

Choose which preposition needs to go in each gap.

a	na/w/do/z/za	Jestem _____ emeryturze.
b	na/w/do/zz/a	Idę _____ domu.
c	na/w/do/z/za	Siedzi _____ domu.
d	na/w/do/z/za	Dziękuję _____ wszystko.
e	na/w/do/z/za	Chcemy zamówić stolik _____ restauracji.
f	na/w/do/z/za	_____ którą godzinę?
g	na/w/do/z/za	_____ widzenia.
h	na/w/do/z/za	_____ zobaczenia.
i	na/w/do/z/za	Chciałbym się spotkać _____ tobą.
j	na/w/do/z/za	Chcielibyśmy się spotkać _____ hotelu.

Exercise 12

Translate the following into English.

a Nasze (*our*) dzieci chciałyby zwiedzić Poznań.
b Chciałabyś zrobić zakupy?
c Potrzebujemy pomocy.
d Potrzebują samochodu.
e Chciałybyśmy zamówić taksówkę.
f Czekamy na przewodnika.
g Państwo czekają na taksówkę?
h Czekają na pana.

Exercise 13

Put the conversational snippets below into an order that makes sense.

a Proszę bardzo.
b A ja poproszę kawę.
c Poproszę sernik i lody.
d Słucham panie?
e Dzień dobry paniom.

Exercise 14

Translate the following into English.

a Jem obiad.
b Jemy bigos.
c Chciałby zobaczyć Londyn.
d Chciałaby pani pójść na obiad?
e Nie lubię kuchni tajlandzkiej.
f Czy ten obraz jest słynny?

Exercise 15

Translate the following into Polish.

a They all (**wszyscy**) like going to (visiting) museums and galleries.
b Why are you (sir) asking?
c I'd love to.
d This book is not interesting.
e We have a new car.
f He has a hairdressing salon.

Exercise 16

Translate the following into Polish.

a It's a pity that (**że**) you're not allowed to take photos in the gallery.
b You can buy postcards in the museum shop.
c What a beautiful album!
d Go along the corridor, please.
e You have to pay by credit card.
f I'd like to pay by debit card (**karta debetowa**).

Exercise 17

Translate the following into English.

a Kupiłem dwa plakaty i trzy magnesy.
b A ja kupiłam album i cztery zakładki.

c Nie wiem, co tu można kupić.

d Nie wiedzą, że w muzeum nie wolno robić zdjęć.

e Proszę państwa, zaraz (*now, in a moment*) przejdziemy korytarzem do sklepu muzealnego.

f Proszę iść prosto. Sklep jest na lewo.

Exercise 18

Translate the following into English.

a To fascynująca informacja.

b Możemy się spotkać albo w moim hotelu, albo w restauracji.

c Czekam na panią w recepcji.

d Hotel jest niedaleko Rynku.

e Dokąd ten pies idzie?

f Chciałbym być genealogiem i pracować w jakimś (*some/a*) archiwum.

g Chciałbym być fryzjerem i mieć swój własny (*own*) salon.

h Szukam pani biura.

i Szuka pani biura?

Exercise 19

Translate the following into Polish.

a My ancestors come from Wales.

b We've an appointment right next door.

c I'll explain to you why I would like to be an architect.

d What's happened?

e What happened?

f I understand you'd like to be a doctor.

Exercise 20

Translate the following into Polish.

a I'm a colonel.

b I'd like a drink of tea with lemon.

c Do help yourself to biscuits.

d Have you got any relatives in France?
e A distant relative of mine (my distant female relative) lives in Warsaw.
f Can you find the address?
g Will you be able to find the address? (Just translate this as: *Will you find the address?*)

Exercise 21

Translate the following into English.

a Prawie (*nearly*) wszyscy moi przodkowie byli słynni.
b Czy to jest jego portret?
c Ciekaw jestem (*I wonder*), czy znajdzie pani jakichś moich przodków.
d Czy oni wszyscy są naprawdę (*really*) moimi krewnymi?
e Wolisz herbatę z mlekiem czy z cytryną?

Exercise 22

Translate the following into English.

a Jaka jest różnica pomiędzy artylerią a kawalerią?
b Nie przypuszczałem, że jej ojciec był tkaczem.
c To jest portret słynnego malarza. (*This is ambiguous, so give two translations!*)
d Ta tradycja rodzinna ma długą historię.
e W tym starym budynku pracowali kupcy, malarze, złotnicy i tkacze.
f Co państwo robili w archiwum?
g Szukaliśmy przodków tego pana.

Exercise 23

Translate the following into Polish.

a They're Germans.
b What were the Russians and Hungarians doing?
c The Italians were painters.

d The Jews and the French were weavers and goldsmiths.
e I didn't know that the Dutch were soldiers. That's interesting.
f My paternal uncle was a Jew.

Exercise 24

Translate the following into Polish.

a I'd like to have a look at the old prints.
b What kind of manor house is it?
c Here you are, here's a map.
d I have a room with a view of the castle.
e What happened to the hotel?
f What's happened to the shop?
g Can we go to Kraków this afternoon?

Exercise 25

Translate the following into English.

a Niestety, kościół jest kompletnie zrujnowany.
b Państwo mogą ze mną pojechać.
c Nie trzeba mówić o takich rzeczach. (*Loc. pl.*)
d Co się panu stało?
e Otrzymał od króla nagrodę (*prize, reward*).
f Zbudujemy nowy dom.

Exercise 26

Translate the following into English.

a Jak daleko jest Łódź?
b Musi pani zawrócić i pojechać w kierunku (*in the direction*) Wrocławia.
c Przepraszam, jak dojść do fontanny?
d Ta ulica prowadzi do Muzeum Narodowego.
e Dlaczego droga jest zamknięta?
f Był wypadek.

Exercise 27

Translate the following into Polish.

a He's standing near the church.
b Turn right and then go straight ahead.
c Where does this (street/road) lead to?
d We'll turn back.
e Have you (sir) ever been there?
f Have you (madam) ever been to Nowe Szkoty?
g Have you (ladies and gentlemen) ever been to Kraków?

Exercise 28

Translate the following into English.

a Proszę iść do salonu.
b Idziemy do salonu.
c Ta biblioteka jest ogromna.
d To (jest) ogromna biblioteka.
e Chciałbym mieć dwie łazienki i trzy pokoje gościnne.
f Siedzi w ogrodzie.
g Chodźmy do ogrodu.
h Proszę wejść do kaplicy.
i Klucz wisi na wieszaku.

Exercise 29

Translate the following into Polish.

a What a lovely room!
b The garden was in front of the house.
c It looks as if there used to be a larder here.
d There were stables by the house.
e Let's go in(side).
f Why is the door open?
g Why are the doors open?
h From here you can see a small chapel.
i Five bedrooms. That's a lot.

Key to the exercises

Unit 1

Exercise 1
a Polką
b Irlandczykiem
c pracowita
d zajęty

Exercise 2
a zmęczona
b Anglikiem
c emerytką

Exercise 3
Masculine: samochód, telefon, dom, autobus, tramwaj, tulipan
Feminine: lampa, herbata, kobieta, mapa
Neuter: radio, dziecko, piwo

Exercise 4
a Dzień dobry.
b Bardzo mi miło.
c Jestem Maria Grajewska.
d Proszę wejść.
e Proszę usiąść.
f Czy jest pan zmęczony?
g Nie jestem głodny (*masc.*)/głodna (*fem.*)
h Czy jest pan Szkotem, Anglikiem czy Polakiem?
i Czym się pani zajmuje?
j Jestem emerytką/Jestem na emeryturze.
k Jestem Anglikiem/Angielką i jestem prywatnym detektywem.

Exercise 5
a Polką
b Anglikiem

c emerytką

d Proszę wejść

Exercise 6

a Bardzo mi miło.

b Dziękuję.

c Tak, trochę.

d Jestem na emeryturze./Jestem emerytem *(masc.)*/emerytką *(fem.)*

Unit 2

Exercise 1

a To jest mój pies, Toffee.

b To jest bardzo dobry pies.

c Czy to jest twoja rodzina?

d Tak, to jest moja żona i córka.

e Jest bardzo ładna.

f Molly jest studentką.

g Studiuje medycynę.

h Kto to jest?

i To jest mój dziadek, Jakub.

j Czy to jest twoja mama?

k Co to jest?

l To jest moja rodzina.

Exercise 2

a ładna

b córka

c pies

d medycynę

e pies

Exercise 3

Examples:

To jest moja mama, żona, siostra, córka.

To jest mój tato (ojciec), mąż, brat, syn.

Exercise 4

a To jest mój ojciec.
b (Ona) Studiuje medycynę.
c Bardzo mi miło.
d Nie, to (jest) dobry pies.

Unit 3

Exercise 1

a Mam rodzinę w Polsce.
b Mam problem.
c Mam ochotę na herbatę.
d Czy masz/ma pan/ma pani jakieś kontakty w Archiwum?
e Nie mam czasu.
f Mam dużo czasu.
g Czy ma pani jakieś dokumenty?
h Moja córka ma dobrą pracę.
i Mam psa, Rexa.
j Mam dwadzieścia lat.

Exercise 2

a Chyba tak.
b Jaki problem?
c Tak, mam dużo czasu.
d Tak, mam (ochotę).

Exercise 3

a Nie mam czasu.
b Nie mam rodziny.
c Nie mam dobrej pracy.
d Mój syn nie jest architektem.
e Nie mam pieniędzy.
f Andrew nie ma dokumentów i fotografii.
g Nie mają psa.
h To nie jest mój ojciec.
i Ona nie jest bardzo ładna.

Exercise 4

a Kim pani jest/Czym się pani zajmuje?

b Kto to jest?

c Czy to jest twój/pana/pani ojciec?

d Czy masz/ma pan/ma pani dokumenty?

e Czy Azor to (jest) zły pies?

Unit 4

Exercise 1

a Muszę już iść.

b Dlaczego musisz/musi pan/musi pani iść?

c Ona musi wrócić do jej hotelu.

d Muszę zadzwonić do domu.

e Musisz zwiedzić/zobaczyć Londyn.

f Musimy spotkać się znowu.

g Bardzo chętnie.

h O tak, koniecznie.

Exercise 2

a Bardzo chętnie.

b O tak, koniecznie.

c Szkoda.

d Tak, mam.

e Nazywam się ...

Exercise 3

a iść

b rzeczy

c pieniądze

d zwiedzić/zobaczyć

e spraw

Unit 5

Exercise 1

a Dziękuję za spotkanie.

b Chciałbym znaleźć moją rodzinę.

c Chciał(a)bym zamówić stolik.

d Poproszę nazwisko.

e Co słychać?

f Na którą godzinę?

g Na siódmą trzydzieści.

h Chciał(a)bym spotkać się z tobą/z panem/z panią.

i Chciał(a)bym znaleźć pewne dokumenty.

Exercise 2

a Nie chciałbym zamówić stolika.

b Nie chciałabym kupić przewodnika.

c Nie muszę zobaczyć Wawelu.

d Nie mam konia.

e Nie chciałbym wymienić pieniędzy.

f Nie muszę zrobić zakupów.

g Nie jestem głodny.

Exercise 3

a Jakiej pomocy?

b Poproszę adres.

c Nie, jestem Szkotem.

d O której godzinie?

Exercise 4

a w Krakowie

b Wawelu

c informacji

d psa

e stolik

f przewodnik

Unit 6

Exercise 1

a Poproszę kawę.

b Poproszę sernik.

c Chciał(a)bym zapłacić rachunek.

d Wykluczone.

e Jesteś moim gościem.
f Poproszę widokówkę.
g Poproszę znaczek lotniczy do Wielkiej Brytanii.
h Ile płacę?

Exercise 2

a Poproszę herbatę.
b Chciał(a)bym herbatę.
c Poproszę kawę.
d Chciał(a)bym kawę.
e Poproszę znaczek.
f Chciał(a)bym kupić znaczek.
g Poproszę przewodnik.
h Chciał(a)bym kupić przewodnik.
i Poproszę rachunek.
j Chciał(a)bym zapłacić rachunek.

Exercise 3

a **emerytem** – wrong gender; should be **emerytką**.
b **Polką** – wrong gender; should be **Polakiem**.
c **kawa** – wrong case; should be (acc.) **kawę**.
d **znaczek** – wrong noun; should be **stolik**.
e **jestem** – wrong verb; should be **Mam**.
f **herbata** – wrong case; should be **herbatę**.
g **kupić** – wrong verb; should be **zwiedzić** or **zobaczyć**.

Exercise 4

a Proszę.
b Poproszę kawę.
c Wykluczone. Jesteś moim gościem.
d Dwa złote pięćdziesiąt groszy.

Unit 7

Exercise 1

a Jestem trochę głodny/głodna.
b Czy lubisz/lubi pan/lubi pani polską kuchnię?
c Tak, lubię polskie piwo.

d Co chciał(a)byś/chciałby pan/chciałaby pani zobaczyć/zwiedzić w Krakowie?

e Chciał(a)bym zobaczyć Rynek i Sukiennice.

f Czy lubisz/lubi pan/lubi pani zwiedzać muzea i galerie?

g Lubię obrazy Leonarda da Vinci.

h W Krakowie jest słynny obraz Leonarda.

i Czy chciał(a)byś/chciałby pan/chciałaby pani zobaczyć ten obraz?

j Lubię kuchnię chińską, ale nie lubię kuchni indyjskiej.

Exercise 2

a pić

b czekoladę

c słuchać

d tańczyć

e zwiedzać

f oglądać

g grać

Exercise 3

1 e, **2** c, **3** h, **4** j, **5** l, **6** b or m, **7** b or m, **8** i, **9** k, **10** g, **11** f, **12** a, **13** d

Exercise 4

a Tak, lubię.

b Nie, nie lubię.

c Chciał(a)bym zobaczyć kościół Mariacki.

d Lubię kuchnię polską i (kuchnię) włoską.

Unit 8

Exercise 1

a telefony

b komputery

c samochody

d stoliki

e słowniki

f ręczniki

g murarze

Exercise 2

a Czy wolno robić zdjęcia w muzeum?
b Przykro mi, ale nie wolno.
c Szkoda.
d Czy można kupić przewodnik w sklepie muzealnym?
e Co jeszcze można tam kupić?
f Można tam kupić książki i zakładki.
g Gdzie jest sklep?
h Czy trzeba wyjść z muzeum?
i Sklep jest na parterze.
j Trzeba iść prosto.
k Przepraszam, czy można zapłacić kartą kredytową?
l Przykro mi/Niestety nie można.
m Co jeszcze warto kupić?

Exercise 3

a Nie, nie wolno.
b Na parterze.
c W sklepie muzealnym.
d Nie wiem; trzeba zapytać.
e Chciałbym zwiedzić Wawel.
f Bardzo chętnie.

Exercise 4

a zobaczyć/obejrzeć/zrobić
b sklep
c kartą kredytową
d parterze
e kupić
f korytarzem
g schodach
h prawo, lewo

Unit 9

Exercise 1

a Słucham
b Mówi John.
c Co słychać?

d Dobrze, dziękuję.

e Mam interesującą wiadomość.

f Do zobaczenia.

g Kiedy możemy spotkać się?

h Gdzie możemy spotkać się?

i Co się stało?

j Dokąd idziemy?

k Chodźmy.

l Kto to jest?

m Kto to jest Ewa?

n Ewa to moja przyjaciółka.

o Ewa pracuje w Archiwum.

p Ewa pracuje w Krakowie.

Exercise 2

a Na ulicę Sienną.

b O czwartej.

c Do zobaczenia.

d Tuż obok Rynku.

e Ewa to moja przyjaciółka.

f Chyba tak.

g Naprawdę?

Exercise 3

a stało

b drodze

c idziemy

d mówi

e wiadomość/informację

f spotkamy

g przyjaciółka

h Archiwum/w Krakowie

Unit 10

Exercise 1

a poniedziałek – masc.

b wtorek – masc.

c środa – fem.

d czwartek – masc.
e piątek – masc.
f sobota – fem.
g niedziela – fem.

Exercise 2
a pracowała
b kupił
c widzieliśmy
d byli

Exercise 3
a Czy byłeś/byłaś/był pan/była pani w Muzeum Czartoryskich?
b Tak, byłem/byłam tam wczoraj.
c Czy widziałeś/widziałaś/widział pan/widziała pani obraz Leonarda?
d Twój/pana/pani przodek był Szkotem.
e Nazywał się Robert Sutherland.
f Czy napijesz się/pan napije się/pani napije się herbaty?
g Kawę z mlekiem (po)proszę.
h Proszę poczęstować się herbatnikami.
i Moja daleka krewna/mój daleki krewny mieszka w Polsce.
j Czy masz/ma pan/ma pani adres?
k Jeszcze nie.

Exercise 4
a cytryną
b mieszka
c herbatnikami
d przodka
e Muzeum
f pisarką
g uczoną
h malarzem

Exercise 5
a Tak, z mlekiem proszę.
b Jeszcze nie.
c Tak, byłem tam wczoraj.

d Tak, jest fascynujący.

e Robert Sutherland był moim przodkiem.

f Był pułkownikiem artylerii w służbie polskiego króla.

Unit 11

Exercise 1

a kobiety

b doniczki

c pielęgniarki

d przyjaciółki

e kanapki

f marmolady

g reklamy

h broszury

i kanapy

j komody

k sukienki

Exercise 2

a Szkoci mieszkali w Polsce.

b Nie wiedziałem/wiedziałam, że Anglicy mieszkali w Polsce.

c Nie tylko Anglicy, ale także Francuzi i Holendrzy.

d To bardzo interesujące/ciekawe

e Czym się zajmowałeś/zajmowałaś?

f Byłem lekarzem/Byłam lekarką.

g A twoja/pana/pani matka?

h Była archiwistką.

i A twój/pana/pani ojciec?

j Mój ojciec był adwokatem.

k Mój dziadek był żołnierzem.

l To rodzinna tradycja.

Exercise 3

a Był lekarzem.

b Tak, byli żołnierzami, kupcami i tkaczami.

c Włosi byli architektami i malarzami.

d Byli prawnikami.

e Nie, oni są Niemcami.

Exercise 4

 a archiwistką
 b prawnikiem
 c mieszkali
 d ciekawe
 e prawnikiem
 f cytryną
 g był
 h biura

Unit 12

Exercise 1

 a Czy mogę obejrzeć fotografie?
 b To jest mapa Krakowa.
 c To jest fotografia dworu.
 d Robert Sutherland otrzymał duży majątek od króla.
 e Czy mogę zobaczyć dwór?
 f Niestety dwór jest kompletnie zrujnowany.
 g Czy możesz/może pan/może pani pojechać ze mną?
 h Czy możemy pojechać tam dziś po południu?
 i Tak, oczywiście.

Exercise 2

 a Tak, oczywiście.
 b To jest stary sztych z widokiem dworu.
 c Moja krewna tam mieszka.
 d Dobrze.
 e Niestety, nie możemy.
 f Tak, proszę bardzo/Tak, oczywiście.

Exercise 3

 a książkę
 b kartą kredytową
 c dworem
 d majątek
 e obrazy
 f zbudował
 g autobusem

Unit 13

Exercise 1

a Jak daleko jest Kraków?

b Niedaleko

c Czy byłeś/byłaś/był pan/była pani tam kiedyś?

d Tak, wiele lat temu.

e Przepraszam, co się stało?

f Wypadek.

g Trzeba zawrócić.

h Jak dojechać do wsi/wioski?

i Dokąd idziesz/jedziesz?

j Proszę skręcić w prawo przy kościele.

k Droga prowadzi do starego dworu.

l Droga jest zamknięta.

Exercise 2

a zamknięta

b stało

c prosto

d skręcić

e zawrócić

f zachód

g kiedyś

Exercise 3

a Niedaleko.

b Nie, ale chciałbym tam pojechać.

c Wypadek.

d Do Nowych Szkotów.

e Do starego dworu.

f Obok kościoła.

Unit 14

Exercise 1

a dwa ogrody

b siedem ogrodów

c trzy klucze
d dziewięć kluczy

Exercise 2
a dwie łazienki
b sześć łazienek
c cztery kaplice
d dziesięć kaplic

Exercise 3
a dwa okna
b siedem okien
c cztery pióra
d osiem piór

Exercise 4
a Jaki piękny widok!
b To był kiedyś piękny dom.
c Dom ma salon, jadalnię i sypialnię.
d Czy jest łazienka w domu?
e Wygląda, że dom miał także ogród.
f Ogród był za domem.
g Mała kaplica stała w parku.
h Jaka szkoda, że dom jest zrujnowany.
i Czy masz/ma pan/ma pani klucz?
j Chodźmy/Wejdźmy do środka.
k Drzwi są otwarte.

Exercise 5
a Tak, (jest) bardzo piękny.
b Miał sześć sypialni.
c Tak, była łazienka.
d Kaplica, biblioteka, ogród i park.
e Ogród był za domem
f Czy masz/ma pan/ma pani klucz?
g Nie, chciałbym mieszkać w pałacu.

Exercise 6

a klucz
b drzwi
c sypialni
d widok
e łazienka
f kuchnia
g stajnie
h kaplica

Unit 15

Exercise 1

a Czy wierzysz w horoskopy?
b Tak, wierzę w horoskopy.
c Nie, nie wierzę.
d Jaki jest twój znak?
e Będziesz podróżować do Krakowa z przyjacielem/przyjaciółką.
f Znajdziesz nowych przyjaciół.
g Wygram milion na loterii.
h Chciał(a)bym wygrać milion na loterii.
i Co za nonsens!
j Co za niespodzianka!
k Coś podobnego!
l Nie rozumiem.
m Co ty tu robisz/Co pan/pani tu robi?

Exercise 2

a Nie, nie wierzę.
b Byk.
c Tak, chciałbym.
d Coś podobnego!
e Mówi, że będę podróżować i znajdę nowych przyjaciół.
f Nie do wiary!

Exercise 3

a znak
b loterii
c pomyślne
d napięciu
e wiadomość
f właścicielem
g nonsens

Test yourself revision exercises

Exercise 1

a Danuta Kosińska
b Tomasz Dąbrowski
c Andrzej Kosiarski
d Ewa Kowalska
e Krzysztof Jakubowski
f Edward Paderewski
g Maria Słomczyńska
h Barbara Jaworska

Exercise 2

a I am Janusz Kowalczyk.
b Pleased to meet you.
c I'm not Polish. I'm English.
d I've got Polish roots.
e Andrzej is retired.
f Maria is Polish.
g What do you do (for a living)?

Exercise 3

a man
b woman
c man
d woman
e man
f woman

Exercise 4

a I'm a doctor (male).
b He's hungry (male).
c She's hard working (female).
d She's Scottish.
e She's busy (female).
f She's a student.
g He's an actor.
h He's a doctor.

Exercise 5

a mój pies
b mój kot
c moja rodzina
d to jest
e medycynę
f studentką
g to
h ładna
i ładną dziewczyną
j przystojny
k to

Exercise 6

a rodzinę
b rodziny
c jaki
d jaki
e żadna
f jakieś
g dokumenty/fotografie
h na
i adresu
j adres
k na
l rencistką
m rencista
n samochodu

Exercise 7

a I am able to/I can.
b They understand.
c We don't understand.
d Are you (plural) able to?
e I have!
f You have!
g What's your (first) name, madam?
h I've got a good job.
i They have documents.

Exercise 8

a What do you have to do, sir?
b I must/have to return home.
c We must/have to meet again.
d We must/have to.
e I must/have to exchange the money.
f No, you don't have to, sir.
g I want to unpack.
h Absolutely?

Exercise 9

a musi
b muszą
c musisz
d musimy
e pan
f spotkać
g zwiedzić

Exercise 10

a On przeprasza.
b Oni/one przepraszają.
c (My) przepraszamy.
d Dlaczego ona nie przeprasza?

Exercise 11

a na
b do

c w
d za
e w
f na
g do
h do
i z
j w

Exercise 12

a Our children would like to (sight)see Poznań.
b Would you like (*fem.*) to do some shopping?
c We need help.
d They need a car.
e We (*fem./pl.*) would like to book/order a taxi.
f We are waiting for the guide.
g Are you (ladies and gentlemen) waiting for a taxi?
h They are waiting for you, sir.

Exercise 13

a Dzień dobry paniom.
b Słucham panie.
c Poproszę sernik i lody.
d A ja poproszę kawę.
e Proszę bardzo.

Exercise 14

a I'm eating dinner.
b We are eating hunter's stew.
c He would like to see London.
d Would you like to go (out) for dinner, madam?
e I don't like Thai cuisine.
f Is this painting famous?

Exercise 15

a Wszyscy zwiedzają muzea i galerie.
b Dlaczego pan pyta?
c Bardzo chętnie.
d Ta książka nie jest interesująca.

e Mamy nowy samochód.
f On ma salon fryzjerski.

Exercise 16
a Szkoda, że nie wolno robić zdjęć w galerii.
b Można kupić widokówki w sklepie muzealnym.
c Jaki piękny album!
d Proszę iść korytarzem.
e Musisz zapłacić kartą kredytową.
f Chciał(a)bym zapłacić kartą debetową.

Exercise 17
a I bought (*masc.*) two posters and three (fridge) magnets.
b And I bought (*fem.*) an album (coffee table book) and four bookmarks.
c I don't know what you (one) can do here.
d They don't know you can't take photos in the museum.
e Ladies and gentlemen, in a moment we will go along the corridor to the museum shop.
f Please go straight ahead. The shop is on the left.

Exercise 18
a It's fascinating information.
b We can meet either in my hotel or in a restaurant.
c I'm waiting for you (madam) in reception.
d The hotel is not far from the Market Square.
e Where is this dog going?
f I (*masc.*) would like to be a genealogist and work in an Archive.
g I (*masc.*) would like to be a hairdresser and have my own salon.
h I'm looking for your (madam) office.
i Are you (madam) looking for an office?

Exercise 19
a Moi przodkowie pochodzą z Walii.
b Jesteśmy umówieni tuż obok.
c Wytłumaczę ci, dlaczego chciał(a)bym być architektem.
d Co się stało?
e Co się stało?
f Rozumiem, że chciałbyś być lekarzem/chciałabyś być lekarką.

Exercise 20

a Jestem pułkownikiem.
b Chciał(a)bym napić się herbaty z cytryną.
c Poczęstuj się herbatnikami.
d Czy masz jakichś krewnych we Francji?
e Mój daleki kuzyn (moja daleka kuzynka) mieszka w Warszawie.
f Czy możesz znaleźć adres?
g Czy znajdziesz adres?

Exercise 21

a Nearly all my ancestors were famous.
b Is this his portrait?
c I wonder if you find any of my ancestors.
d Are they all really my relatives?
e Do you prefer tea with milk or with lemon?

Exercise 22

a What's the difference between the artillery and the cavalry?
b I didn't suppose her father was a weaver.
c This is a portrait of the famous painter/this is a portrait by the famous painter.
d This family tradition has got a long history.
e In this old building merchants, painters, goldsmiths and weavers were working.
f What did you (ladies and gentlemen) do in the Archive?
g We were looking for the ancestors of this gentleman.

Exercise 23

a Oni są Niemcami/One są Niemkami.
b Co robili (czym się zajmowali) Rosjanie i Węgrzy?
c Włosi byli malarzami.
d Żydzi i Francuzi byli tkaczami i złotnikami.
e Nie wiedziałem/wiedziałam, że Holendrzy byli żołnierzami.
  To ciekawe.
f Mój stryjeczny wuj był żydem.

Exercise 24

a Chciał(a)bym obejrzeć stare sztychy.
b Jaki to dwór?

c Proszę, tu jest mapa.
d Mam pokój z widokiem zamku/na zamek.
e Co się stało z hotelem?
f Co się stało ze sklepem?
g Czy możemy pojechać do Krakowa dziś po południu?

Exercise 25
a Unfortunately, the church is completely ruined.
b You (ladies and gentlemen) can go with me.
c You don't need to talk about such things.
d What happened to you (sir)?
e He received a prize from the King.
f We will build a new home.

Exercise 26
a How far is Łódź?
b You have to turn round and go towards Wrocław.
c Excuse me, how to get/go to the fountain?
d This street leads to the National Museum.
e Why is the road closed?
f There was an accident.

Exercise 27
a On stoi koło kościoła.
b Proszę skręcić w prawo iść i potem prosto.
c Dokąd prowadzi ta ulica?
d Zawrócimy.
e Czy był pan kiedyś tam?
f Czy była pani kiedyś w Nowych Szkotach?
g Czy były panie kiedyś w Krakowie?

Exercise 28
a Please go to the salon.
b We are going to the salon.
c This library is huge.
d This is a huge library.
e I (*masc.*) would like to have two bathrooms and three guest rooms.
f S/he sits/is sitting in the garden.

g Let's go to the garden.
h Please go into the chapel.
i The key hangs/is on the hook.

Exercise 29

a Jaki cudowny pokój!
b Ogród był przed domem.
c Wygląda na to, że była tu kiedyś spiżarnia.
d Stajnie były przy/obok domu.
e Chodźmy/Wejdźmy do środka.
f Dlaczego drzwi są otwarte?
g Dlaczego drzwi są otwarte?
h Stąd widać małą kaplicę.
i Pięć sypialni. To dużo.

Polish–English vocabulary

a *and* (with a change of participant), *and/but*
A to? *And (what about) this?*
adresu (adres) *address*
adwokatem (adwokat) *barrister*
albumy (album) *albums*
Anglicy (Anglik) *English people*
Anglikiem (Anglik) *Englishman*
ani … ani … *neither … nor …*
architektami (architekt) *architects*
architektem (architekt) *architect*
archiwum *archive(s)*
archiwistką (archiwistka) *archivist (female)*
aż do kościoła (kościół) *right as far as the church*

bardzo chętnie *very happily, willingly, would love to*
bardzo *very*
Bardzo mi miło. (ja, miły) *Pleased to meet you.*
bez znaczenia (znaczenie) *meaningless, without significance*
będziesz podróżować (być, podróżować > popodróżować) *you'll travel/be travelling*
bibliotekę (biblioteka) *library*
bigos traditional Polish cabbage stew known as *hunter's stew*
być *to be*

byk *bull/Taurus*
byli (być) *they were*
był kiedyś *used to be, was once*
był pan (być) *you have been*
byłem (być) *I was*

chętnie (chętny) *willingly, with pleasure*
chodź (chodzić > pochodzić) *come on*
chodźmy (chodzić > pochodzić) *let's go*
chodźmy do środka (chodzić, środek) *let's go in(side)*
chyba *I think, I suppose*
ciekawe (ciekawy) *interesting*
co się stało (stawać się > stać się) *what's happened*
co słychać? *how are things? what's new?*
Co ty powiesz! (co, ty, powiedzieć) *Fancy that!*
co za *what sort of, what*
córka *daughter*
czas na + acc. *time for*
cześć *hi*
czwarta (czwarty) *four o'clock (the fourth hour)*
czy word used to introduce a yes/no question; *or*
Czym się pan/pani zajmuje? *What do you do for a living?/ What are you doing?*

dama *lady (poetic)*
detektywem (detektyw) *detective*
dla + gen. *for, for the sake of*
dla ciebie (dla, ty) *for you*
dlaczego *why*
długa rodzinna tradycja (długi, rodzinny, tradycja) *long family tradition*
do + gen. *to*
do małego skrzyżowania (mały, skrzyżowanie) *up to a small crossroads*
do mojego biura (do, mój, biuro) *to my office*
do sklepu (sklep) *to the shop*
do starego dworu (do, stary, dwór) *to the old manor house*
do widzenia (widzenie; widzieć > zobaczyć) *goodbye (till we see each other)*
do Wielkiej Brytanii (Wielka Brytania) *to Great Britain*
do zobaczenia (zobaczenie; widzieć > zobaczyć) *see you*
dobrą pracę (dobra, praca) *a good job*
dobry *good*
dobrze (dobry) *OK, correctly, well, right*
dojechać do + gen. **(dojeżdżać > dojechać)** *get to, come up to, reach*
dokąd *where (to)*
dokumenty (dokument) *documents*
domu (dom) *home, house*
droga *way, path, road*

drzwi *doors*
dużo *a lot*
duży majątek *big estate, fortune*
dwa pięćdziesiąt *two fifty*
dwa pokoje gościnne (pokój gościnny) *two guest rooms*
dworu (dwór) *of the manor house*
dziadek *grandfather*
dzieci (dziecko) *children*
dziennikarzem (dziennikarz) *journalist*
dzień *day*
dzień dobry (dzień, dobry) *hello, good morning, good afternoon*
dziękuję za (dziękować > podziękować *thank you for*
dziś *today*

emerytką (emerytka) *retired woman*

fantastyczną wiadomość (fantastyczna wiadomość) *a fantastic piece of news*
fascynującą informację (fascynujący, informacja) *a fascinating bit of information*
fotografie (fotografia) *photographs*
Francuzi (Francuz) *French (people)*

galerie (galeria) *gallery*
gdzie *where*
genealogiem (genealog) *genealogist*

głodny *hungry*
gościem (gość) *guest*
gronostaj *ermine*

herbatę (herbata) *tea*
herbatnikami (herbatnik)
  biscuits
herbaty (herbata) *some tea*
Holendrzy (Holender) *Dutch
  people*
horoskopy (horoskop)
  horoscopes
hotelu (hotel) *hotel*

i *and*
imię *first name, Christian name*
**interesującą wiadomość
  (interesujący, wiadomość (f.))**
  an interesting piece of news
inżynierami (inżynier)
  engineers
iść *to go*
itd. *etc.*

jadalnię (jadalnia) *dining room*
jak daleko (jak, daleko) *how far
  away*
jaką (jaki) *what, what sort of*
jaki *what kind of, what a*
jakichś krewnych (jakiś krewny)
  any relatives
jest (być) *he/she/it is*
jestem *I'm*
**jesteśmy umówieni (umówiony;
  umawiać się > umówić się)**
  *we've got an appointment,
  arrange a meeting*
jeszcze *still, besides, more, yet*

jutro *tomorrow*
już *already, now*

**kartą kredytową (karta
  kredytowa)** *by credit card*
kiedyś *ever, at any time,
  one day*
kilka *a few, several*
kim (kto) *what (in terms of
  profession)*
kim pani była (kto, pani, być)
  *what were you, what did
  you do*
klucz *key*
kompletnie (kompletny)
  completely
koniecznie *necessarily, absolutely
  (must)*
kontakty (kontakt) *contacts*
korytarzem (korytarz) *along the
  corridor*
książki (książka) *books*
Kto to jest? *Who is it (this)?*
Kto? *Who?*
Która godzina? (który, godzina)
  What's the time (which hour?)
kuchnia *kitchen, cuisine, food*
kuchnię (kuchnia) *kitchen,
  cuisine*
kupcami (kupiec) *merchant*
kupić (kupować > kupić) *buy*

lekarzem (lekarz) *doctor*
**lody kawowe (lód, lody,
  kawowy)** *coffee ice cream*
lotniczy *airmail*
ładna (ładny) *pretty*
łosiczka *(little) weasel*

ma (mieć) *(s/he/it) has*

magnesy (magnes) *(fridge) magnets*

malarzami (malarz) *painters*

mała kaplica (mały, kaplica) *a small chapel*

Mama *Mum*

mapa *map*

medycynę (medycyna) *medicine*

męża (mąż) *husband*

mieszkali (mieszkać) *lived*

milion *a million*

mogę (móc) *I can, I may*

moi przodkowie (mój, przodek) *my ancestors, my forebears*

moja (mój) *my (f.)*

można *it's possible to*

mój *my* (used with masc. nouns)

mówi (mówić > powiedzieć) *is speaking, speaks*

musi pan *you must, sir*

muszę (musieć) *I must/I have to*

Muszę już iść. *I must go now./I have to go now.*

muzea (muzeum) *museums*

na + loc. *(located) on, at*

na emeryturze (na, emerytura) *on a pension, retired*

na którą godzinę (która godzina) *what time for, when for*

na loterii (loteria) *in a/the lottery*

na parterze (parter) *on the ground floor*

na prawo od *on/to the right of*

napijecie się + gen. (napijać się > napić się) *you'll have a drink of, you'll have something to drink, have enough to drink*

naprawdę *really*

narodowe (narodowy) *national*

nazwiska (nazwisko) *surname*

nazywał się (nazywać się > nazwać się) *his (sur)name was*

nie *no, not*

nie ma za co *not at all, no problem, don't mention it, it's OK*

nie trzymaj nas (trzymać, my) *don't keep us*

nie wiem (wiedzieć) *I don't know*

niedaleko + gen. *not far away (from)*

niedaleko Krakowa *near, not far from Kraków*

Niemcy (Niemiec) *Germans*

niestety *unfortunately, sadly*

no *well, then, yes*

nonsens *rubbish, nonsense*

notariuszem (notariusz) *notary*

nowych przyjaciół (nowy przyjaciel) *new friends*

o czwartej *at four*

o której *at what time*

obejrzeć (oglądać > obejrzeć) *(have a) look at*

obiad *lunch, dinner*

obok Rynku *next to the Market Square*

obrazy (obraz) *paintings*

oczywiście (oczywisty) *certainly, obviously*

od domu (dom) *from the house*

od Krakowa *from Kraków*

od króla (król) *from the king*

odkryć (odkrycie) *of discoveries*

odkryjesz (odkrywać > odkryć) *you'll discover*

**odwiedzisz (odwiedzać >
odwiedzić)** *you'll visit*
ogród *garden*
ojciec *father*
ojej *oh dear*
**otrzymał (otrzymywać >
otrzymać)** *he received*
otwarte (otwarty) *open*

**pana daleka krewna (pan,
daleki krewny)** *a distant female
relation*
pani *Madam/Mrs/Ms, lady, your
(to a woman)*
pani mąż *your husband, madam*
panu (pan) *Sir/Mr, gentleman*
park *park*
pewnie (pewny) *certainly, surely*
pieniądze (pl.) *money*
pies *dog*
piękny widok *beautiful, fine view*
piwo *beer/lager*
plakaty (plakat) *posters*
planeta *planet*
po + loc. *after, along, by*
po drodze (po, droga) *on the
way*
po schodach (schody) *by the
stairs, along the stairs*
pochodzą z + gen. **(pochodzić)**
come, originate from
pocztówki (pocztówka) *postcard*
podróży (podróż) *of travel, of
journey(s)*
pojechać (jechać > pojechać) *go
(other than on foot)*
pojechać drogą na + acc. *take
the road to*
pokój *room, peace*

Polką (Polka) *Polish woman*
polskiego króla (polski król) *of
the Polish king*
pomyślne (pomyślny)
favourable, positive
po południu *in the afternoon,
this afternoon*
poproszę (prosić > poprosić)
please (extra polite), I'll ask for
portret *portrait*
potem *then, next, afterwards*
**potrzebuję pomocy
(potrzebować** + gen., **pomoc)**
I need help
poza tym (poza, to) *besides
(that)*
**pracuje (pracować >
popracować)** *she works*
prawie *almost*
prawnikami (prawnik) *lawyers*
priorytet *priority*
problem *problem*
prosto (prosty) *straight (on)*
proszę (prosić > poprosić)
please
proszę poczęstować się + instr.
**(częstować się > poczęstować
się)** *please help yourselves to*
**prowadzi do (prowadzić >
poprowadzić)** *leads, takes you to*
prywatnym (prywatny) *private*
przejść (przechodzić > przejść)
*go/come through, go/come
across*
**przepraszam (przepraszać >
przeprosić)** *sorry, excuse me,
I apologize*
przeszłość *the past*
przewodnik *guide(book)*

przy figurce (przy, figurka) *by a small statue*
przyjaciółka *(female) friend*
przyjaźni (przyjaźń) *of friendship*
przykro mi (przykry, ja) *I'm sorry*
przypuszczałem (przypuszczać > przypuścić) *suppose, think, imagine*
pułkownikiem (pułkownik) *colonel*
pytać o + acc. (pytać > zapytać) *ask about*

rachunek *bill*
recepcja *reception (desk)*
restauracja (f.) *restaurant*
robić zdjęcia (robić > zrobić; zdjęcie) *take photographs*
robili (robi > zrobić) *were doing, were making*
rodzina *family*
rodzinne (rodzinny) *family (adjective)*
rodziny (rodzina) *family*
Rosjanie (Rosjanin) *Russians*
rozpakować się (rozpakowywać się > rozpakować się) *get unpacked*
rozumiem (rozumieć > zrozumieć) *I understand, I gather*
rynek *market*

salon *sitting room*
sernik *cheesecake*
skręcić w prawo (skręcać > skręcić) *turn right*
słucham (słuchać) *hello, I'm listening, pardon?, listen, Can I help you?*

słucham państwa *Can I help you?* (literally: *I'm listening to you, ladies and gentlemen*)
słychać + acc. ... *can be heard*
słynny *famous*
spiżarnię (spiżarnia) *larder*
spotkać się *meet, get together* **(spotykać się > spotkać się)**
spotkanie *meeting, get-together*
spraw (sprawa) *thing, matter, problem*
stajnie (stajnia) *stables*
stary dom *an old house*
stary sztych *an old print*
stąd *from here*
stolik (masc.) *table in a restaurant, small table*
stryj *paternal uncle*
studentką (studentka) *female student*
studiuje (studiować) *s/he studies, is a student of*
Sukiennice (pl.) *the Cloth Hall*
syna (syna) *son*
sześć sypialni (sypialnia) *six bedrooms*
szkockie korzenie (szkocki, korzeń) *Scottish roots*
szkoda *pity, shame, damage, waste*
szkoda, że *it's a pity (that)*
Szkotem (Szkot) *Scot (sman)*
szuka + gen. (szukać > poszukać) *is looking for*
szuka pan rodziny (szukać > poszukać, rodzina) *you're looking for relatives*

ta droga *that road, the path*
tak *yes*
także *also*
też *too, also, as well*
tkaczami (tkacz) *weavers*
to jest (być) *this is, it's*
To żaden problem. *It's no problem at all.*
trochę *a little bit*
trzeba *one needs to*
trzy łazienki (łazienka) *three bathrooms*
tuż obok + gen. *right next door (to)*

usiąść (siadać > usiąść) *to sit down*
uskrzydlonych rycerzy (uskrzydlony rycerz) *of winged knights*
uwierzycie (wierzyć > uwierzyć) *you'll believe*

w + acc. *into, to*
w + loc. *in*
w artylerii (artyleria) *in the artillery*
w dół *downwards*
w kawalerii (kawaleria) *in the cavalry*
w krainie (w, kraina) *in the land* (poetic)
w lewo *left/on the left*
w napięciu (napięcie; napinać > napiąć) *in suspense*
w Polsce (Polska) *in Poland*
w sferę (w, sfera) *into the area, sphere, region*

w sklepie muzealnym *in the museum shop* **(sklep, muzealny)**
w służbie (służba) *in the service*
w twoim hotelu (twój hotel) *at/in your hotel*
warto *worth*
wczoraj *yesterday*
wejść *come in/go in*
weszła (wchodzić > wejść, w) *she has moved into*
Węgrzy (Węgier) *Hungarians*
wiary (wiara) *belief, faith*
widać + acc. *can be seen*
widokówka *postcard*
wiedziałem (wiedzieć) *I knew* (said by a man)
wiele lat (wiele, rok) *many years*
wierzyć w + acc. *believe in* **(wierzyć > uwierzyć)**
więc *so*
właścicielem (właściciel) *owner*
Włosi (Włoch) *Italians*
wolno *it's allowed, one may*
wrócić do + gen. **(wracać > wrócić)** *come/go back to*
wsi (wieś) *of a village*
wszystko *everything, all*
wygląda, że (wyglądać) *it looks as if*
wygram (wygrywać > wygrać) *I'll win*
wyjść (wychodzić > wyjść) *go out, come out*
wykluczone (wykluczony; wykluczać > wykluczyć) *excluded, out of the question*

wymienić (wymieniać > wymienić) *change, exchange, enumerate*

wypadek *accident*

wytłumaczę ci (tłumaczyć > wytłumaczyć, ty) *I'll explain to you*

z + instr. *with*

z cukrem (cukier) *with sugar*

z cytryną (cytryna) *with lemon*

z dziesięć lat (rok/lato) *ten years or so*

z Ewą (Ewa) *with Ewa*

z mlekiem (mleko) *with milk*

z muzeum + gen. *from/out of the museum*

z tobą (ty) *with you*

z widokiem (widok) *with a view*

za + acc. *(moving) behind*

za + instr. *(located) behind*

za domem (dom) *behind the house*

zadzwonić (dzwonić > zadzwonić) *ring, telephone*

zakładki (zakładka) *bookmarks*

załatwić (załatwiać > załatwić) *deal with; do; settle*

zamknięta (zamknięty; zamykać > zamknąć) *closed*

zamówić (zamawiać > zamówić) *to order*

zapłacić (płacić > zapłacić) *pay*

zapłacić za + acc. (płacić > zapłacić) *pay for*

zapytać (pytać > zapytać) *ask*

zasięgnąć informacji (zasięgać > zasięgnąć, informacje (pl.)) *get some information*

zawrócić (zawracać > zawrócić) *turn round, turn back*

złotnikami (złotnik) *goldsmiths*

zły *bad, angry, malicious* (here: *aggressive*)

zmęczony (męczyć > zmęczyć) *tired*

znaczek *stamp*

znaczki (znaczek) *stamps*

znajdę (znajdować > znaleźć) *I'll find (it)*

znajdziesz (znajdować > znaleźć) *you'll find*

znak (Zodiaku) (znak, Zodiak) *sign (of the Zodiac)*

znaleźć (znajdować > znaleźć) *find*

znowu *again*

zobaczyć (widzieć > zobaczyć) *see*

zrujnowany (rujnować > zrujnować) *ruined, in ruins*

zwiedzić (zwiedzać > zwiedzić) *visit, go sightseeing in*

zwykły *ordinary, usual*

żaden *none*

żołnierzami (żołnierz) *soldiers*

żona *wife*

Żydzi (Żyd) *Jews*

English–Polish vocabulary

absolutely (must) **koniecznie**

accident **wypadek**

address **adres**

after **po** + loc.

afternoon: in the ~, this ~ **po południu**

afterwards **potem**

again **znowu**

airmail **lotniczy**

albums **albumy (album)**

all **wszystko**

allowed: it's ~ **wolno**

almost **prawie**

along **po** + loc.

already **już**

also **także; też**

ancestors: my ~ **moi przodkowie (mój, przodek)**

and **i**

And (what about) this? **A to?**

and (change of participant) **a**

angry **zły**

apologize: I ~ **przepraszam (przepraszać > przeprosić)**

appointment: we've got an ~ **jesteśmy umówieni (umówiony; umawiać się > umówić się)**

architect; ~s **architektem (architekt); architektami**

archive **archiwum**

archivist (female: she is ~) **archiwistką (archiwistka)**

area: into the ~ **w sferę (w, sfera)**

artillery: in the ~ **w artylerii (artyleria)**

as well **też**

ask **zapytać (pytać > zapytać)**

ask about **pytać o** + acc. **(pytać > zapytać)**

ask for: I'll ~ **poproszę (prosić > poprosić)**

at **na** + loc.

away: how far ~ **jak daleko (jak, daleko)**

bad **zły**

barrister **adwokat**

bathrooms: three ~ **trzy łazienki (łazienka)**

be: to ~; used to ~ **być; był kiedyś**

bedrooms: six ~ **sześć sypialni (sypialnia)**

been: you have ~ **był pan (być)**

beer **piwo**

behind: (moving); (located) **za** + acc.; **za** + instr.

belief **wiara**

believe: you'll ~ **uwierzycie (wierzyć > uwierzyć)**

believe in **wierzyć w** + acc. **(wierzyć > uwierzyć)**

besides; ~ (that) **jeszcze; poza tym (poza, to)**

bill **rachunek**

biscuits **herbatniki, herbatnik**

bookmarks **zakładki (zakładka)**
books **książki (książka)**
bull **byk/Taurus**
but **a**
buy **kupić (kupować > kupić)**
by **po** + loc.

can: I ~ **mogę (móc)**
can I have? **poproszę (prosić >**
   poprosić)
cavalry: in the ~ **w kawalerii**
   (kawaleria)
certainly **oczywiście (oczywisty),**
   pewnie (pewny)
change **wymienić (wymieniać >**
   wymienić)
chapel: a small ~ **mała kaplica**
   (mały, kaplica)
cheesecake **sernik**
children **dzieci (dziecko)**
closed **zamknięta (zamknięty;**
   zamykać > zamknąć)
Cloth hall **Sukiennice** (pl.)
coffee ice cream **lody kawowe**
   (lód, lody, kawowy)
colonel: I am/was ~ ; he is/was a ~
   pułkownikiem (pułkownik)
come across **przejść**
   (przechodzić > przejść)
come back to **wrócić do** + gen.
   (wracać > wrócić)
come from: they ~ **pochodzą z** +
   gen. **(pochodzić)**
come in **wejść**
come on: you ~ **chodź (chodzić >**
   pochodzić)
come out **wyjść (wychodzić >**
   wyjść)

come through **przejść**
   (przechodzić > przejść)
come up to **dojechać do** + gen.
   (dojeżdżać > dojechać)
completely **kompletnie**
   (kompletny)
contacts **kontakty (kontakt)**
correctly **dobrze (dobry)**
corridor: along the ~ **korytarzem**
   (korytarz)
credit card: by ~ **kartą kredytową**
   (karta kredytowa)
crossroads: up to a small ~ **do**
   małego skrzyżowania (mały,
   skrzyżowanie)
cuisine: I like ~ **kuchnię (kuchnia)**

damage **szkoda**
daughter **córka**
day; one ~ **dzień; kiedyś**
deal with **załatwić (załatwiać >**
   załtwić)
dear: oh ~ **ojej**
detective: I (masc) am/was ~;
   he is/was ~ **detektywem**
   (detektyw)
dining room: it had a ~ **jadalnię**
   (jadalnia)
dinner **obiad**
discover: you'll ~ **odkryjesz**
   (odkrywać > odkryć)
discoveries: of ~ **odkryć (odkrycie)**
do **załatwić (załatwiać >**
   załtwić)
doctor: I (masc) am/was ~;
   he is/was ~ **lekarzem (lekarz)**
documents **dokumenty**
   (dokument)

dog **pies**

doing: were ~ **robili (robić >**
 zrobić)

door: right next ~ *(to)* **tuż obok**
 + gen.

doors **drzwi**

downwards **w dół**

drink: you'll have a ~ *of, you'll have*
 something to ~*, have enough to*
 ~ **napijecie się + gen. (napijać**
 się > napić się)

Dutch people **Holendrzy**
 (Holender)

engineers: they (virile) are/were ~
 inżynierami (inżynier)

English people **Anglicy (Anglik)**

Englishman **Anglikiem (Anglik)**
 I (masc.) am/was ~
 he is/was ~

ermine **gronostaj**

estate: big ~ **duży majątek**

etc. **itd.**

ever **kiedyś**

everything **wszystko**

exchange **wymienić (wymieniać**
 > wymienić)

excluded **wykluczone**
 (wykluczony; wykluczać >
 wykluczyć)

excuse me **przepraszam**
 (przepraszać > przeprosić)

explain: I'll ~ *to you* **wytłumaczę**
 ci (tłumaczyć > wytłumaczyć, ty)

faith **wiara**

family **rodzina; rodzinne**
 (rodzinny); rodziny (rodzina)

famous **słynny**

Fancy that! **Co ty powiesz!**
 (co, ty, powiedzieć)

far: not ~ *away (from)* **niedaleko**
 + gen.

father **ojciec**

favourable **pomyślne**
 (pomyślny)

few: a ~ **kilka**

find; you'll ~*; I'll* ~ *(it)* **znaleźć**
 (znajdować > znaleźć);
 znajdziesz; znajdę

food: good ~ **dobra kuchnia**

for; ~ *you* **dla + gen.; dla ciebie**
 (dla, ty)

fortune **duży majątek**

four: at ~ **o czwartej**

four o'clock (the fourth hour)
 czwarta (czwarty)

French (people) **Francuzi**
 (Francuz)

friend (female) **przyjaciółka**

friends: new ~*;* **nowi przyjaciele,**
 nowych
 you'll meet new ~ **przyjaciół**
 (nowy przyjaciel)

friendship: of ~ **przyjaźni**
 (przyjaźń)

from here **stąd**

galleries **galerie (galeria)**

garden **ogród**

genealogist: I am/was ~
 genealogiem (genealog)
 s/he/is/was ~

gentleman/sir: thank you ~ **panu**
 (pan)

Germans **Niemcy (Niemiec)**

get to **dojechać do** + gen.
  (dojeżdżać > dojechać)
get together **spotkać się**
  (spotykać się > spotkać się)
get-together **spotkanie**
go: to ~; I must ~ now.; **iść;**
  Muszę już iść.; chodźmy *let's*
  ~; let's ~ in(side) **(chodzić >**
  pochodzić);chodźmy do
  środka (chodzić >, środek)
go (other than on foot) **pojechać**
  (jechać > pojechać)
go across **przejść (przechodzić >**
  przejść)
go back to **wrócić do** + gen.
  (wracać > wrócić)
go in **wejść**
go out **wyjść (wychodzić >**
  wyjść)
go through **przejść (przechodzić**
  > przejść)
goldsmiths **złotnikami (złotnik)**
good **dobry**
good afternoon **dzień dobry**
  (dzień, dobry)
good morning **dzień dobry**
  (dzień, dobry)
goodbye (till we see each other)
  do widzenia (widzenie;
  widzieć > zobaczyć)
grandfather **dziadek**
Great Britain: to ~ **do Wielkiej**
  Brytanii (Wielka Brytania)
ground floor: on the ~ **na**
  parterze (parter)
guest **gościem (gość)**
guest room **pokój gościnny**
guide (book) **przewodnik**

happily: very ~ **bardzo chętnie**
has: (s/he/it) ~ **ma (mieć)**
have to **musieć**
heard: ... can be ~ **słychać** + acc.
hello **dzień dobry (dzień,**
  dobry), słucham (słuchać)
help: Can I ~ you?; I need ~;
  słucham państwa; potrzebuję
  please ~ yourselves to **pomocy**
  (potrzebować + gen., **pomoc);**
  proszę poczęstować się + instr.
  częstować się > poczęstować
  się, pomoc
hi **cześć**
home **(dom)**
horoscopes **horoskopy (horoskop)**
hotel; at/in your ~ **(hotel); w**
  twoim hotelu (twój hotel)
house; an old ~; behind the ~;
  domu (dom); stary dom; za
  domem *from the ~* **(dom); od**
  domu (dom)
how are things? **co słychać?**
Hungarians **Węgrzy (Węgier)**
hungry **głodny**
husband; your ~ **(mąż);**
  pani/twój mąż

I'm **jestem**
in **w** + **locative**
information: a fascinating bit
  of ~; get some ~ **fascynującą**
  informację (fascynujący,
  informacja); zasięgnąć
  informacji (zasięgać >
  zasięgnąć, informacje (pl.))
interesting **ciekawe (ciekawy)**
into **w** + acc.

is: he/she/it ~ **jest (być)**
it's **to jest (być)**
Italians **Włosi (Włoch)**

Jews **żydzi (żyd)**
job: (I have) a good ~ **dobrą**
  pracę (dobra, praca)
journalist: he is/was~
  dziennikarzem (dziennikarz)
journey: of ~(s) **podróży (podróż)**

keep: don't ~ us **nie trzymaj nas**
  (trzymać, my)
key **klucz**
kind: what ~ of **jaki**
king: from the ~; of the Polish ~
  od króla (król); polskiego króla
  (polski król)
kitchen **kuchnię (kuchnia)**
knew: I ~ **wiedziałem (wiedzieć)**
knights: of winged ~
  uskrzydlonych rycerzy
  (uskrzydlony rycerz)
know: I don't ~ **nie wiem**
  (wiedzieć)
Kraków: from ~ **od Krakowa**

lady **dama (poetic), pani**
lager **piwo**
land: in the ~ (poetic) **w krainie**
  (w, kraina)
larder **spiżarnia**
lawyers: we/they are/were ~
  prawnikami (prawnik)
leads you to **prowadzi do**
  (prowadzić > poprowadzić)
left **(w) lewo**
lemon: with ~ **z cytryną (cytryna)**

library **biblioteka**
listen **słuchać**
listening: I'm ~ **słucham**
little: a ~ bit **trochę**
lived: they ~ **mieszkali**
  (mieszkać)
look: (have a) ~ at **obejrzeć**
  (oglądać > obejrzeć)
looking: you're ~ for relatives;
  szuka pan rodziny (szukać > is
  ~ for **poszukać, rodzina); szuka**
  + gen. (szukać > poszukać)
looks: it ~ as if **wygląda, że**
  (wyglądać)
lot: a ~ **dużo**
lottery: in a/the ~ **na loterii**
  (loteria)
love: would ~ to **bardzo chętnie**
lunch **obiad**

Madam **pani**
magnets: (fridge) ~ **magnesy**
  (magnes)
making: were ~ **robili (robi >**
  zrobić)
malicious **zły**
manor house: of the ~; to **dworu**
  (dwór); do starego dworu
  the old ~ **(do, stary, dwór)**
map **mapa**
market **rynek**
matter **sprawa**
may: I ~; one ~ **mogę (móc);**
  wolno
meaningless **bez znaczenia**
  (znaczenie)
medicine: s/he studies ~
  medycynę (medycyna)

meet **spotkać się** (spotykać się >
   spotkać się)
meeting; arrange a ~ **spotkanie;
   jesteśmy umówieni**
   (umówiony; umawiać się >
   umówić się)
mention: don't ~ it **nie ma za co**
merchant **kupiec**
milk: with ~ **z mlekiem** (mleko)
million **milion**
money **pieniądze** (pl.)
more **jeszcze, więcej**
moved: has ~ into **weszła**
   (wchodzić > wejść, w)
Mr **panu** (pan)
Mrs **pani**
Ms **pani**
Mum **Mama**
museum: from/out of the ~; ~s
   **z muzeum; w sklepie
   muzealnym** (sklep, muzealny);
   muzea (muzeum)
must: you ~; I ~; one ~ **musi pan;
   muszę** (musieć)
my (used with masc. nouns); (f.)
   mój; moja

name: first/Christian ~; **imię;
   nazywał się** (nazywać się >
his (sur)~ was **nazwać się**)
national **narodowe** (narodowy)
near Kraków **niedaleko Krakowa**
necessarily **koniecznie**
needs to: one ~ **trzeba**
neither … nor … **ani … ani …**
new: what's ~? **co słychać?**
news: a fantastic piece of ~;
   (fantastyczna wiadomość);

an interesting piece of ~
   (interesujący, wiadomość (f.))
next; ~ to the Market Square
   potem; obok; obok Rynku
no **nie**
none **żaden**
nonsense **nonsens**
not **nie**
not at all **nie ma za co**
notary **notariuszem**
   (notariusz)
now **już, teraz**

obviously **oczywiście**
   (oczywisty)
office: to my ~ **do mojego biura**
   (do, mój, biuro)
OK; it's ~ **dobrze** (dobry); **nie
   ma za co**
on (located) **na** + loc.
on the way **po drodze** (po,
   droga)
open **otwarty**
or **czy**
order: to ~ **zamówić**
   (zamawiać > zamówić)
ordinary **zwykły**
originate from **pochodzić z**
   + gen.
owner: I am/he is ~ **właścicielem**
   (właściciel)

painters: we/you/they are ~
   malarzami (malarz)
paintings **obrazy** (obraz)
pardon? **słucham** (słuchać)
park **park**
past: the ~ **przeszłość**

paternal uncle **stryj**
path; the ~ **droga; ta droga**
pay; ~ for **zapłacić (płacić >**
zapłacić); zapłacić za + acc.
(płacić > zapłacić)
peace **pokój**
pension: on a ~ **na emeryturze**
(na, emerytura)
photographs; take ~ **fotografie**
(fotografia); robić zdjęcia
(robić > zrobić; zdjęcie)
pity; it's a ~ that **szkoda;**
szkoda, że
planet **planeta**
please **proszę (prosić >**
poprosić)
please (extra polite) **poproszę**
(prosić > poprosić)
Pleased to meet you. **Bardzo mi**
miło. (ja, miły)
pleasure: with ~ **chętnie (chętny)**
Poland: in ~ **w Polsce (Polska)**
Polish woman: I am/she is ~ **Polką**
(Polka)
portrait **portret**
positive **pomyślny**
possible: it's ~ to **można**
postcard **pocztówki (pocztówka);**
widokówka
posters **plakaty (plakat)**
pretty **ładna (ładny)**
print: an old ~ **stary sztych**
priority **priorytet**
private **prywatny**
problem; It's no ~ at all.; no ~
problem, spraw (sprawa);
To żaden problem.; nie ma
za co

question: out of the ~
wykluczone (wykluczony;
wykluczać > wykluczyć)

reach **dojechać do** + gen.
(dojeżdżać > dojechać)
really **naprawdę**
received: he ~ **otrzymał**
(otrzymywać > otrzymać)
reception (desk) **recepcja**
reception room **pokój gościnny**
region: into the ~ **w sferę (w,**
sfera)
relation: a distant female ~
daleka krewna (daleki
krewny)
relatives: any ~ **jakichś krewnych**
(jakiś krewny)
restaurant **restauracja** (f.)
retired; retired woman **na**
emeryturze (na, emerytura);
emerytką (emerytka)
right; ~ as far as the church;
dobrze (dobry); aż do kościoła
on/to the ~ of **(kościół); na**
prawo od
ring **zadzwonić (dzwonić >**
zadzwonić)
road; take the ~ to; that ~ **droga;**
pojechać drogą na + acc.;
ta droga
room **pokój**
rubbish **nonsens, śmiecie**
ruined **zrujnowany (rujnować >**
zrujnować)
ruins: in ~ **zrujnowany**
(rujnować > zrujnować)
Russians **Rosjanie (Rosjanin)**

sadly **niestety**

sake: for the ~ *of* **dla** + gen.

Scot (sman) **Szkotem (Szkot)**

Scottish roots **szkockie korzenie (szkocki, korzeń)**

see; ~ *you* **zobaczyć (widzieć > zobaczyć); do zobaczenia (zobaczenie; widzieć > zobaczyć)**

seen: can be ~ **widać** + acc.

service: in the ~ **w służbie (służba)**

settle **załatwić (załatwiać > załatwić)**

several **kilka**

shame: it's a ~ **szkoda**

shop: to the ~ **do sklepu (sklep)**

sightseeing: go ~ *in* **zwiedzić (zwiedzać > zwiedzić)**

sign (of the Zodiac) **znak (Zodiaku) (znak, Zodiak)**

Sir **pan**

sit down: to ~ **usiąść (siadać > usiąść)**

sitting room **salon**

so **więc**

soldiers; we/you/they are ~ **żołnierzami (żołnierz)**

son **syn**

sorry; I'm ~ **przepraszam (przepraszać > przeprosić); przykro mi (przykry, ja)**

sort: what ~ *of* **jaką (jaki)**

speaking: is ~ **mówi (mówić > powiedzieć)**

speaks **mówi (mówić > powiedzieć)**

sphere: into the ~ **w sferę (w, sfera)**

stables **stajnie (stajnia)**

stairs: by/along the ~ **po schodach (schody)**

stamp; ~*s* **znaczek; znaczki (znaczek)**

statue: by a small ~ **przy figurce (przy, figurka)**

stew: (traditional Polish cabbage stew known as *hunter's stew*) **bigos**

still **jeszcze**

straight (on) **prosto (prosty)**

student: female ~; *is a* ~ *of* **studentką (studentka); studiuje (studiować)**

studies: s/he ~ **studiuje (studiować)**

sugar: with ~ **z cukrem (cukier)**

suppose; I ~*ed* **przypuszczałem (przypuszczać > przypuścić); chyba**

surely **pewnie (pewny)**

surnames **nazwiska (nazwisko)**

suspense: in ~ **w napięciu (napięcie; napinać > napiąć)**

table (in a restaurant)/small ~ **stolik** *(m)*

takes you to **prowadzi do (prowadzić > poprowadzić)**

tea; Can I have some ~ **herbatę (herbata); herbaty (herbata)**

telephone **telefon** (noun), **zadzwonić** (verb) **(dzwonić > zadzwonić)**

ten years or so **z dziesięć lat (rok/lato)**

thank you for **dziękuję za**

then **no, potem**

thing **rzecz, sprawa**

think; I thought (masc.)
  przypuszczałem (przypuszczać
  > przypuścić); chyba

this is **to jest (być)**

time: at any ~; at what ~; **kiedyś;**
  o której; na którą godzinę
  what ~ for; What's the ~?; ~
  for **(która godzina); Która**
  godzina? (który, godzina);
  czas na + acc.

tired **zmęczony (męczyć >**
  zmęczyć)

to **do + gen., w + acc.**

today **dziś**

tomorrow **jutro**

too **też**

tradition: long family ~ **długa**
  rodzinna tradycja (długi,
  rodzinny, tradycja)

travel: of ~; you'll ~/be ~ing
  podróży (podróż); będziesz
  podróżować (być, podróżować
  > popodróżować)

turn right **skręcić w prawo**
  (skręcać > skręcić)

turn round/back **zawrócić**
  (zawracać > zawrócić)

two fifty **dwa pięćdziesiąt**

understand: I ~ **rozumiem**
  (rozumieć > zrozumieć)

unfortunately **niestety**

unpacked: get ~ **rozpakować**
  się (rozpakowywać się >
  rozpakować się)

usual **zwykły**

very **bardzo**

view: beautiful/fine ~; with a ~
  piękny widok; z widokiem
  (widok)

village: of a ~ **wsi (wieś)**

visit; to ~ **zwiedzić**
  (zwiedzać > zwiedzić);
  odwiedzisz (odwiedzać >
  odwiedzić)

was: I ~ (masc.) **byłem (być)**

waste **strata**

way **droga**

weasel, (little)
  łosiczka

weavers; **tkacze; tkaczami**
  (tkacz)

we/you/they are/were ~

well **dobrze (dobry); no**

were: they ~ **byli (być)**

what; ~ (in terms of profession)
  jaką (jaki); kim (kto)

What are you doing? **Co robisz/**
  co pan/pani robi?

What do you do for a living?
  Czym się pan/
  pani zajmuje?

what sort of **co za**

What were you doing?/What
  did you do (for a living)?
  Kim pani była?
  (kto, pani, być)

What's happened? **Co się stało?**
  (stawać się > stać się)

when for **na którą godzinę**
  (która godzina)

where **gdzie**

where (to) **dokąd**

Who is it (this)? **Kto to jest?**
Who? **Kto?**
why **dlaczego**
wife **żona**
willingly **bardzo chętnie**
win: I'll ~ **wygram (wygrywać >
  wygrać)**
with; ~ Ewa; ~ you **z + instr.;
  z Ewą (Ewa); z tobą (ty)**

works: she ~ **pracuje
  (pracować > popracować)**
worth **warto**

years: many ~ ago **wiele lat
  temu (wiele, rok)**
yes **tak**
yesterday **wczoraj**
yet **jeszcze**

Polish language game

To play the game you will need:

- a board
- a dice
- a counter
- four sets of cards marked in different colours: blue, green, yellow and purple.

How to play

The object of the game is to reach the finish or meta square.

The dice is thrown and the counter is moved the relevant number of spaces. The counter will land on a coloured square* or a white square with an instruction. The player must then draw a card of the same colour as the square landed on or follow the instruction.

- Cards marked in blue contain a translation task.
- Cards marked in green test your grammatical knowledge.
- Cards marked in yellow refer to communication tasks.
- Cards marked in purple refer to general knowledge questions.

You can write the correct answer to the question on the reverse of the card. Should you land on a grey square, you may choose a card of any colour. Play continues with the throw of the dice and a card is drawn at the end of each turn.

*Please note: because the book is printed in black and white the colours on the board are marked with letters:

- B – blue
- Gn – green
- Gy – grey
- P – purple
- Y – yellow

META	B99	Back to 5	P97	Gy96	Y95	B94	Back one	P92	GY91
Y81	B82	Gn83	P84	Forward two	Y86	B87	Gn88	Forward one	Gy90
Y80	B79	Back two	P77	Gy76	Y75	Back to 28	Gn73	P72	Back two
Y61	B62	Gn63	P64	Back one	Y66	B67	Gn68	P69	Gy70
Forward one	B59	Gn58	P57	Gy56	Forward to 59	B54	Back two	P52	Gy51
Y41	B42	Gn43	Forward one	Gy45	Y46	B47	Gn48	P49	Back to 30
Y40	B39	Forward five	P37	Gy36	Forward one	B34	Back two	P32	Gy31
Y21	B22	Gn23	P24	Forward three	Y26	B27	Gn28	P29	Gy30
Y20	Back to 16	Gn18	P17	Gy16	Y15	B14	Back to start	P12	Gy11
START	B2	Gn3	Go to 10	Gy5	Y6	Back two	Gn8	P9	Gy10

Taking it further

Since the accession of Poland to the European Union in 2004 there has been a tremendous growth in the number of books, magazines, dictionaries, computer software and web sites, etc. to enable you to learn Polish and find out more about Poland.

It is impossible to list everything, but the following list should provide a good starting point:

Other language courses by Hodder Education

Speak Polish with confidence by Joanna Michalak-Gray
Complete Polish by Nigel Gotteri and Joanna Michalak-Gray

Dictionaries

Collins Easy Learning Polish Dictionary
DK Polish–English Visual Bilingual Dictionary
Pocket Oxford – PWN Polish Dictionary
Oxford – PWN Polish–English, English–Polish Dictionary (2 vol.)

About Poland

If you are interested in the history of Poland, then the following books may be of interest to you:

God's Playground by Norman Davies, OUP Oxford, 2nd revised edition 2005. *Heart of Europe* by Norman Davies, Oxford Paperbacks, updated edition 2001. *Rising '44* by Norman Davies, Pan Books, new edition 2004.

The Polish Way by Adam Zamoyski, Hippocrene Books, Inc, new edition 1993, *Poland. A Traveller's Gazetteer* by Adam Zamoyski, John Murray Publishers Ltd, 2001. *A Traveller's History of Poland* by John Radzilowski, Chastleton Travel, 2007. *The Long Walk* by Sławomir Rawicz, Robinson

Publishing, 2007. *The Polish Officer* by Alan Furst, HarperCollins Publishers Ltd, new edition, 1998. *The Bronski House* by Philip Marsden, HarperPerennial, new edition, 2005. *For Your Freedom and Ours, The Kościuszko Squadron* by Lynne Olson & Stanley Cloud, Arrow Books Ltd, new edition, 2004. *A Country in the Moon* by Michael Moran, Granta Books, 2008.

Studying Polish in Poland

If you would like to study Polish in Poland then the Internet is the best source of information. Kraków, Warsaw, Łódź, Gdańsk, Poznań, Wrocław, Katowice and Lublin are all big university towns with well established Polish language schools. The Internet will also enable you to find information about new privately owned schools.

Information online

The Internet is the largest source of information about Poland and here you will be able to find tourist information, newspapers, magazines, radio broadcasts, Polish recipes, family genealogical information, Polish music, etc.

Rzeczpospolita is the largest Polish daily newspaper with a good online edition. (www.rp.pl).

Poland.pl is a good starting point to search for general information about Poland.

The recent large influx of Poles to the UK has resulted in a new wave of Polish shops, cafés, restaurants and delicatessens opening in most British towns. All major supermarkets stock Polish food products.

POSK – *Polski Ośrodek Społeczno Kulturalny* (Polish Social and Cultural Centre) in Hammersmith in London offers a library, a bookshop, a theatre, a gallery and a restaurant.